Political issues in Ireland today

Edited by
Neil Collins

Manchester University Press
Manchester and New York

Distributed exclusively in the USA and Canada by St. Martin's Press

Published by Manchester University Press
Oxford Road, Manchester M13 9NR, UK
and Room 400, 175 Fifth Avenue, New York, NY 10010, USA

Distributed exclusively in the USA and Canada
by St. Martin's Press, Inc., 175 Fifth Avenue, New York,
NY 10010, USA

British Library Cataloguing-in-Publication Data
A catalogue record for this book is available from the British Library

Library of Congress Cataloging-in-Publication Data

Political issues in Ireland today / edited by Neil Collins.
   p. cm. — (Politics today)
  ISBN 0–7190–3769–7. — ISBN 0–7190–3770–0 (pbk.)
  1. Ireland—Politics and government—1949– 2. Northern Ireland—
Politics and government—1969– 3. Political planning—Ireland.
4. Political planning—Northern Ireland. I. Collins, Neil.
II. Series: Politics today (Manchester, England).
JN1428.P65 1994
941.50824—dc20   93–40665

ISBN 0 7190 3769 7 *hardback*
    0 7190 3770 0 *paperback*

Typeset in Great Britain
by The Midlands Book Typesetting Company

Printed in Great Britain
by Bell & Bain Ltd, Glasgow

Contents

Tables and figures

Tables

Figures

Preface

This edited volume has been produced in response to requests from students and teachers for an introduction to public policy issues in both the Republic of Ireland and Northern Ireland. All the contributors have become aware that despite a large body of specialist material, there is no readily accessible and comparative study available.

As is in the nature of an edited volume, many people in each of the universities were involved in its production. They all deserve the authors' thanks. Particular acknowledgement must be made, however, to Stephen Kelly, Loretta Fullerton and George McAllister, who each had a hand in assembling, typing and correcting the final manuscript. The book also owes a great deal to the diligence and perseverance of Bill Jones, the series editor, and Richard Purslow, the editorial director of Manchester University Press.

Contributors

Susan Baker is a lecturer in public administration at the Erasmus University in Rotterdam. She has published extensively on environmental issues in Northern Ireland and other parts of Europe.

Leslie Carswell, lecturer in public administration at the University of Ulster, researches in health policy and management. He is currently examining the impact of GP fund-holding on the quality of health care provision.

Neil Collins is Reader in Public Administration at Magee College, University of Ulster. He has written extensively on Irish politics and co-authored (with Frank McCann) *Irish politics today* (MUP).

John Coolahan is Professor of Education at the National University of Ireland. He is a leading authority on education in the Republic of Ireland and has published extensively on his subject.

Douglas Hamilton is principal research officer at the Northern Ireland Economic Council. He is one of Northern Ireland's foremost experts in industrial development.

Richard Haslem, Head of the Department of Public Administration at University College Cork, was formerly Limerick County Manager.

Dennis Kennedy was until recently Head of Office at the EC representation in Belfast. Dr Kennedy, a former editor of the *Irish Times*, is an expert on constitutional developments in Northern Ireland and offers regular commentaries on developments there through academic and mass media channels.

Colin Knox, Senior Lecturer in Public Administration at the University of Ulster, is a former local government officer. His main interests are in policy evaluation. Dr Knox has recently completed a major project on community relations.

Brigid Laffan is the Jean Monnet Professor of European Politics at University College Dublin. She recently published *Integration and Cooperation in Europe* (Routledge).

Denise McAlister is Senior Lecturer in Public Administration at the University of Ulster. She is currently researching systems for ensuring quality in health care.

Joan Moss, Principal Agricultural Economist at the Department of Agriculture, Northern Ireland, and Senior Lecturer at the Queen's University Belfast, is one of Ireland's leading agricultural economists. Her research publications have been a major influence on policy makers in the Republic and Northern Ireland.

Reg North, Senior Lecturer in Education at the University of Ulster, is both a theorist and practitioner in education management. He has contributed widely to the current debate on educational reform in Northern Ireland.

Introduction

This book is about political issues on the island of Ireland. It examines both institutions and policies. The authors are all specialists in aspects of public policy and administration. They have prepared short, balanced and insightful accounts of a range of policies and institutions in the Republic of Ireland and Northern Ireland.

Each of the chapters in this volume highlights both the similarities and contrasts between the two jurisdictions in Ireland. Because the Republic and Northern Ireland share so many environmental, demographic and cultural characteristics, there is a tendency to highlight the contrasts. It is important to note, therefore, as Dennis Kennedy does in Chapter 2, that the two states in Ireland both began in the 1920s with British-type institutions. Even now, despite important constitutional uncertainties, the day-to-day rules and conventions of accountability, administrative practice and citizens' redress are broadly similar.

In Chapter 3, 'Managing Europe', Brigid Laffan analyses the consequences of membership of the European Community (EC) on the political, administrative and judicial systems of the two parts of Ireland. Though their different legal positions as sovereign state and UK region are very important, the development of increased political cohesion and possible economic divergence loom large for both parts of Ireland. Laffan challenges current Irish strategies in the EC and outlines future security and political commitments.

Although they set their account in the context of the variety of European systems, Colin Knox and Richard Haslem describe the two distinct systems of local government within Ireland. Chapter 4 shows most clearly an area in which the two Irish states began with the same institutional framework and have evolved quite differently. Indeed, Chubb, in his seminal work on the government of the Republic, has called its distinctive management system 'perhaps Ireland's major invention in the field of government.'[1] In Northern Ireland, local institutions have changed radically in response to the political turmoil of the past twenty-five years.

In Chapter 5, Denise McAlister's discussion of public expenditure provides the link between the institutional concerns of the opening chapters and the examination of public policy areas which follow. She points to important differences in the methods and patterns of public expenditure in the two jurisdictions. Significantly, however, McAlister finds that in both the Republic and Northern Ireland, public spending is likely to come under increased scrutiny. Economic growth has failed to generate employment and has led to similar fundamental questions about state spending being asked on both sides of the border.

Douglas Hamilton also focuses on the creation of employment in Chapter 6, 'Industrial development'. He discusses the strategies involved in trying to develop industry in Ireland to a level at which it could compete in the international market and, thereby, increase employment. Northern Ireland and the Republic share many of the same problems in this policy area. Hamilton, however, warns that the solutions require developments at a political level.

The most important industry on the island at the moment is agriculture. Joan Moss isolates some of the crucial policy issues for Irish farmers arising from developments in the EC's Common Agricultural Policy. In Chapter 7 she poses questions for policy makers and others about the changing structure of world trade in agricultural products, the renewed emphasis on rural development and the stability of rural society. The shift from an agricultural policy based on price supports to one which gives greater emphasis to direct income aids for farmers has profound implications for Ireland.

The two parts of Ireland display remarkably similar demographic characteristics in that they have relatively young populations, especially in urban centres, as well as large areas in which the elderly predominate. These imbalances lead to special problems in health care provision. Leslie Carswell, in Chapter 8, discusses how the two systems of health and related personal social services are organised to meet Ireland's needs. Northern Ireland has adapted radical reforms in its health services along lines established in Britain. Carswell expects the Republic's system to come under considerable pressure as issues of funding and organisation come to the fore. As in other areas of policy, the example of Britain may also impact directly on the Republic.

One policy area in which the two states have diverged radically, according to Reg North and John Coolahan in Chapter 9, is education. The Northern Ireland system has developed directly in line with England and Wales. It has evolved a highly structured and centrally-directed curriculum and system of pupil testing. The Republic's progress has been more piecemeal and school-based. In addition, the northern school system is heavily segregated in terms of religious affiliation. This situation is not replicated to the same extent in the Republic. The highly selective secondary system in Northern Ireland, in which pupils' educational chances are largely determined by a test at age eleven, has no parallel in the Republic.

As Susan Baker shows in Chapter 10, the island's policy makers face essentially the same environmental problems. They also seek to implement the same EC directives on environmental protection. Ireland has many advantages arising from its geographical position, stable population and pattern of economic development. It is, however, exposed to particular local environmental dangers as well as sharing certain global risks. Baker warns against 'quick fix' technological solutions to global problems and gives a critical assessment of the current institutional safeguards against environmental damage on the island of Ireland.

Many of the issues isolated in this book are the subject of intense political debate in Ireland. Politicians and political parties compete for public attention and support by forming or reflecting popular opinions on education, health, environmental and other issues. They often simplify complex problems by highlighting the basic social values which underpin them. In this way, they allow the electorate to take some part in the decision-making process. Irish politicians and parties are no different from their counterparts in the other democratic countries in fulfilling this role. Chapter 1 looks at recent political developments to see whether or not the party systems in the two parts of Ireland are becoming close to those elsewhere in Europe. In particular, it asks whether a left-right continuum of the kind frequently used to understand party systems in other countries could be usefully applied in either Irish jurisdiction.

Notes

1   Chubb, B. (1988), *Government and politics of Ireland*, Longman, London, p. 288.

Parties and elections: recent developments

Since 1945 Western European politics has been characterised by the commitment of all major political parties and social classes to liberal democracy. The period since 1945 has seen an unparalleled stability in the party systems of Europe. In both Irish jurisdictions the party systems have generally been regarded as exceptional, for while similarly slow to change, neither fits easily into the models most often used for analysis elsewhere in Europe. These models seek to categorise parties into reasonably distinct groupings or 'families' so that while their titles might vary, an understanding can be gained about where an individual party lies in terms of the major divisions of politics. Such political divisions are themselves seen as expressions of social cleavages such as class, religion, regional identity or language. Stable and mature political systems are thought to depend on the efficient expression of the major competing social interests through party competition. Frequently, parties in other European countries are described in terms of their support for socialism, conservatism, liberalism and the like. Such ideological stances can generally be taken to reflect major social divisions of interest.

The particularity of most European party systems can be made more comprehensible by the use of a simple left-right scale. Parties of the left generally present the citizen as a social being and stress the community's responsibility to meet individual needs, possibly through the public ownership of key economic and other resources. Those on the right see minimum government interference as necessary for efficiency and growth. Left- and right-wing parties also differ in their views on the role of the state in relation to the divergent claims of individual and public morality and order. Parties of the centre seek to draw support from both the left and right. This simple model does not imply that the ideological distance from the extremes of left and right is everywhere the same. Similarly, there are European democracies, for example Belgium and the Netherlands, where religions and cultural cleavages have encouraged a multi-party system in which parties may occupy the same position along the left-right continuum but are also, and sometimes principally, identified with a religious or language group.

The parties of Northern Ireland and the Republic seem to defy easy categorisation along the left-right continuum because the main parties owe their origins to historical divisions on constitutional issues, which find few parallels elsewhere. The distinctions between unionist and nationalist parties, or Fianna Fáil and Fine Gael, derive from positions adopted by politicians and their followers 70 and more years ago. As a result, observers often analyse Irish politics in terms of the survival of the existing parties or the potential for new or small parties to exploit those social cleavages which mark out party systems elsewhere. In this chapter, recent electoral and other developments will be examined to assess whether the Republic's or Northern Ireland's party systems are about to change to reflect the kinds of 'family' groups found in other European settings.

Northern Ireland: general elections 1992

The 1992 UK general election in Northern Ireland was fought by 100 candidates from more than 10 different parties. The main players were the traditional parties (listed below), although the Conservative Party in Northern Ireland also contested the election, but only as a minor competitor.

Parties in the 1992 general election in Northern Ireland

Main players
Ulster Unionist Party (UUP)
Democratic Unionist Party (DUP)
Alliance Party of Northern Ireland (ALL)
Social Democratic and Labour Party (SDLP)
Sinn Féin (SF)

Minor players
Conservative Party of Northern Ireland
Workers' Party
Labour and Trade Union
Ulster Popular Unionist Party
Independent Unionist
Natural Law Party

The Alliance Party, though it does support the continuation of the union between Britain and Northern Ireland, claims cross-community support. The unionist parties – principally the DUP and UUP – are straightforwardly in the Protestant and loyalist tradition. The two main unionist parties put up competing candidates in three constituencies in 1992 where a split unionist vote would not let in a nationalist. Elsewhere the unionist parties agreed not to oppose each other. This co-operative stance reflects the two parties' opposition to the Anglo-Irish Agreement[1].

The SDLP is the main constitutional nationalist party and, in common with Sinn Féin, it seeks political change in an all-Ireland context. Sinn Féin calls for a clear commitment from the UK government to a united Ireland and has refused to condemn the terrorism of the Provisional IRA. The SDLP favours peaceful and constitutional change and opposes the violent tactics of all paramilitary forces.

The election manifestos of both the main unionist parties set the scrapping of the Anglo-Irish Agreement as their primary goal. Although they campaigned for a devolved local assembly for Northern Ireland, they emphatically declared the need to retain strong constitutional links with Britain. Away from this central issue, the individual unionist candidates concentrated on constituency issues such as hospital closures, agricultural grants and jobs.

The SDLP offered a broad range of policies, many reflecting its links with socialist parties in other parts of Europe. The SDLP's major emphasis was on the inter-party political negotiations, better known as the 'Brooke Talks'.[2] The commonality of interests between the two parts of Ireland was often stressed by SDLP candidates. For unionists, too great a level of co-operation with the Republic is seen as a grave danger. If, for instance, Ireland was treated as one region for EC purposes, the whole separate existence of the northern state could be undermined. All-Ireland co-operation may be useful in some contexts but only if constitutional criteria are adequately addressed.

Sinn Féin, of course, wishes to see Northern Ireland's present political links with Britain severed. For this party, the central issue in the election was how to facilitate a British withdrawal. The Sinn Féin analysis of Northern Ireland's various social and economic problems identified the partition of Ireland as a root cause. Table 1.1 summarises the result of the general election in Northern Ireland.

West Belfast was the only seat which changed hands. The combined UUP and DUP share of the vote fell slightly (down 1.6 per cent on 1987) and support for the Alliance Party also declined compared to the last UK general election. Support for the SDLP rose by 2.4 per cent while that for Sinn Féin decreased.

The Conservative Party, standing for the first time in a general election in Northern Ireland, took 5.7 per cent of the votes. Its high-profile local leader, Dr Laurence Kennedy, failed to defeat the sitting independent unionist in North Down, although he secured 32 per cent of the vote. The Conservatives have now established themselves as the most important of the minor parties and appear to pose a significant threat to the Alliance Party, which did not reach the 10 per cent share it achieved in 1987.

Table 1.1 *Summary of the result of the 1992 general election in Northern Ireland*

Party	Share of the vote (%)	Change from 1983 (%)	MPs elected	Change from 1987
United Ulster Unionist	34.8	−3.0	9	0
Democratic Unionist	13.1	+1.4	3	0
Ulster Popular Unionist	2.5	0.0	1	0
Alliance	8.7	−1.3	0	0
Social Democratic And Labour	23.5	+2.4	4	+1
Sinn Féin	10.0	−1.4	0	−1
Others[a]	7.4	+2.0	0	0

Note

(a) includes Conservative Party of Northern Ireland, which obtained 5.7% of the total vote, Workers (0.6%), Natural Law (0.3%) and 'Others' (1.2%).

For Sinn Féin, the 1992 election result was a considerable blow. The party's vote has reduced slowly but consistently from 13.4 per cent in 1983 to 10 per cent in 1992. Of more immediate impact was the loss of Sinn Féin's seat. Gerry Adams never actually took his place at Westminster but his status as an MP lent considerable legitimacy to his party outside Ireland.

SDLP pleasure at the gain of West Belfast was almost matched by the party's relief at retaining South Down. Overall, the SDLP's share of the vote rose from 21.1 per cent in 1987 to 23.5 per cent in 1992, and the party's vote averaged nearly 30 per cent in the 13 constituencies it contested.

The Democratic Unionist Party fared badly in the two constituencies where it challenged the UUP. Overall, the DUP's vote rose 1.4 per cent from 1987 but this was because the party fielded three extra candidates in 1992; comparison with the DUP's performance at the local and European elections in 1989 is more telling – and less favourable. Dr Ian Paisley, the DUP leader and MEP, took 30 per cent of the Northern Ireland vote at the European Parliament poll, but the party as a whole is not able to obtain this level of support even though its candidates in 1992 were generally well-known figures.

After the general election, the British Prime Minister, John

Major, changed the Northern Ireland 'team'. Since the Northern Ireland Parliament and government were suspended in March 1972, 'direct rule' from London has been conducted under a UK cabinet minister, supported by several junior colleagues. The new Secretary of State for Northern Ireland, Sir Patrick Mayhew, is committed to continuing the talks process instituted by his predecessor.

Only two weeks after the election, representatives of the UUP, DUP, SDLP and Alliance Party re-opened the inter-party talks about the future of Northern Ireland. In early July, the talks were extended to include the Irish and British governments. The election of a majority government in London and the broad consensus between the major political parties in Dublin offered some grounds to hope for gradual progress towards an agreement. Nevertheless, the talks process formally broke down in November 1992.

The result of the general election of 1992 does not seem to signal a change in the party system in Northern Ireland along new lines. Broadly, the electorate is divided on religious rather than class lines. Nevertheless, in the rhetoric and patterns of support of parties, it is possible to see tendencies to a left/right division within each community. The DUP, in particular, identifies itself as primarily a working-class party, though it does not wish to be labelled 'socialist'. In local government elections it is easier to see that its support is greater in poorer unionist areas. Similarly, the Alliance Party draws the bulk of its votes from solidly middle-class areas and its policy stances are generally of the right. For the Conservative Party, it is too early to say where its support will come from but its members are disproportionately middle class. Dr Kennedy's high poll was in a solidly middle-class constituency. The Conservatives find most of their voters in the Belfast Lough area.

Northern Ireland is represented in the European Parliament (EP) by three members, each of whom has joined one of its groups. Dr Paisley, DUP, is a member of the unattached or independent group, but the other two have joined distinct groups of the left and right. John Hume, SDLP, is a member of the Socialist Group, the EP's largest with 181 of its 518 members, while Jim Nicholson, UUP, has sat with the right-wing European People's Party (EPP) since his election in 1989. EPP is a Christian democratic grouping to which Fine Gael and the British Conservatives also belong. In the EP election of 1989, which was conducted under the single transferable vote (STV) system, of the large surplus of votes for Paisley, 86 per cent was transferred to Nicholson. The rest virtually all went to other non-nationalists.

Within the nationalist community both main parties are of the left but Sinn Féin would claim to be the more radical. Certainly, under the leadership of Gerry Adams, Sinn Féin has increased the socialist content of its rhetoric and its statist orientation. On the other hand, the SDLP is closer to the social democratic tradition which is the major force on the European left in general. In terms of votes, the SDLP is more successful than Sinn Féin in attracting middle-class support.

Republic: presidential election 1990 and general election 1992

The question most frequently asked about the party system in the Republic is how long the 'civil war' division will continue to sustain the two largest parties, Fianna Fáil and Fine Gael. The issue arises because both parties were formed in the wake of the divisions over the Anglo-Irish Treaty of 1921, which led to the Civil War of 1922–23. To the generation which lived through the immediate post-Treaty decades, it is argued, the settlement itself may have been the central issue. Now, however, its salience must surely be very low indeed. Those who ask this question look for signs that a new or revived small party will be able to make a fresh appeal to the electorate based on current realities and achieve major gains in electoral support and Dáil seats. The main issues in the Republic's elections have for a long time been about the management of the economy. It seems most likely, therefore, that any new electoral force would base its challenge on the rival claims made by left- and right-wing parties elsewhere to economic and class self-interest.

There have been several attempts to 'break the civil war mould' of the Republic's system by parties appealing to farmers' interests. However, no farmers' party has seriously challenged the main protagonists. As the rural element of the electorate has declined and changed in character, the focus of those seeking signs of change has been parties which can be defined in terms of the right/left continuum.

One new party, the Progressive Democrats (PDs), formed in 1985, seemed to signal a possible realignment of forces. Though the leadership of the PDs was drawn from former members of the two main parties, its declared intentions were to eschew 'civil war' divisions and offer policy options associated with the European liberal tradition. In the EP, the PDs are part of the Liberal Democratic and Reformist Group. The PDs are decidedly a right-wing party, essentially conservative in economic policy but liberal on 'moral' issues. The new party did remarkably well in 1987 but registered a marked decline in 1989. Ironically, after that election, Fianna Fáil needed to form a coalition with the PDs to retain its hold on office.

The 1987 and 1989 elections also marked a change of fortune for a party of the left. The Workers Party was modelled in 1982 from a splinter group of Sinn Féin into a radical left-wing party. The party was represented in the Dáil by seven deputies in 1989, six of whom broke away to form Democratic Left in March 1992. Democratic Left set itself the objective of working for a democratic pluralist socialist society. It is organised in both Northern Ireland and the Republic.

Democratic Left and the PDs mark the left/right parameters of the Republic's party system. The largest party of the left remains the Labour Party, the oldest in the Dáil. The peculiarity of the Republic's system is illustrated, however, by the fact that throughout the 1980s the combined left-wing vote never exceeded 15 per cent.

The parties of the left consistently maintained that there was a 'natural' constituency for them among the electorate. They pointed to the urbanisation, industrialisation and modernisation of Irish society as well as to the experience of other European countries. The left was also able to recall electoral successes, such as the performance of Labour in the late 1960s, which seemed to bring them to the verge of a dramatic breakthrough. However, each increase in support was followed by disappointing electoral performances. The most recent success for the left, before the general election of 1992, was the defeat of the Fianna Fáil and Fine Gael candidates at the 1990 presidential contest.

Mary Robinson had been a member of the Labour Party but resigned over its policy on the Anglo-Irish Agreement. Nevertheless, the Labour Party was prominent in her nomination and campaign. A victory for Ms Robinson seemed unlikely when she launched her campaign in May 1990. Brian Lenihan (Fianna Fáil), on the other hand, was regarded as a certain winner until the final weeks of the campaign. However, he became embroiled in a controversy about attempts in 1982 by Fianna Fáil to put unconstitutional pressure on the incumbent President Hillery.

Ms Robinson was the candidate backed by the Labour Party with the support of the Workers' Party and other leftist groupings. She had been closely associated with several liberal causes, particularly concerning women's rights. During her campaign she rejected the description 'socialist', though her support for socialism in the past was referred to frequently by her opponents.

The election was held using the single transferable vote system. In the first count it was established that 64.1 per cent of the electorate of 2,471,308 had voted in the ratio 44:39:17 for Lenihan, Robinson and Currie. The elimination of Currie, the Fine Gael candidate, led to the transfer of 76.7 per cent of his vote to Robinson and 13.7 per cent to Lenihan, with 9.5 per cent non-transferable. This resulted in a Robinson victory by 817,830 votes (52.8%) to 731,273 (47.2%). Ms Robinson assumed presidential office on 3 December 1990, the first woman to do so (see table below).

Presidential Election, 1990

Candidate	1st Count	2nd Count
Robinson (Ind)	38.9	52.7
Lenihan (FF)	44.1	47.2
Currie (FG)	17.0	–

For the left wing of Irish politics, Robinson's poll is taken as a sign that attractively- and sensitively-presented campaigns can succeed and break the dominance of the right. The reverberations of their defeat were immediately felt in the two largest parties, Fine Gael and Fianna Fáil, which together held 80 per cent of the seats in Dáil. Both the major Irish parties refuse to define themselves as of the political left or right and both attempt to have a broad populist appeal. The ideological tensions in Fine Gael are largely between economic liberalism and social democracy. The election of Mary Robinson was seen by some in the party as signalling the need for a clearer Fine Gael image as a social democratic party. Others stressed the traditional role of vigorous opposition to Fianna Fáil for the same centrist political constituency.

In her inaugural address President Robinson said, 'We have passed the threshold of a new pluralist Ireland'. Although some hyperbole is expected on such occasions, there are indications that the President's assessment may have been accurate. The next test for the possibility of a long-term change in the party system came in November 1992 with a general election.

The 1992 election was caused by the break-up of the coalition government of Fianna Fáil and the PDs. The relationship between the two parties deteriorated following a change of leadership in Fianna Fáil and a clash over evidence given by the parties' leaders to a parliamentary inquiry into the Republic's beef industry. The parties had also differed sharply over the administration of industrial development policy and the wording of a referendum question on abortion.

The major feature of the election result was that Labour's representation increased from 15 to 33 seats, its greatest representation ever. The party had 23 candidates elected on the first count, including one challenger, Eithne Fitzgerald, who got the highest vote in the state. Overall, the left-wing parties gained 14 seats because Democratic Left lost 2 seats and the Workers Party failed to retain its seat. At the opposite end of the left/right spectrum, the PDs increased their representation from 6 to 10. The main losers were Fianna Fáil and Fine Gael (see Table 1.2).

For Fianna Fáil, the 1992 vote was the party's worst showing in the polls since 1927, the year it entered the Dail for the first time. Much of the criticism in the party was directed at its leader Albert Reynolds, whom, according to opinion polls, many voters blamed for calling an unnecessary election. The Fianna Fáil vote had, however, been declining for several elections; its 39.1 per cent in 1992 was in line with its local election total the previous year.

Table 1.2 *Percentage of first preference votes (and seats) in 1992 and 1989*

Party	1992 % vote	(seats)	1989 % vote	(seats)
Fianna Fail	39.1	(68)	44.1	(77)
Fine Gael	24.5	(45)	29.3	(55)
Labour	19.3	(33)	9.5	(15)
Progressive Democrats	4.7	(10)	5.0	(6)
Democratic Left	2.8	(4)	N/A	N/A
Workers Party	0.7	(–)	5.5	(7)
Independent & others	8.9	(6)	6.6	(6)

Electorate: 2,557.036   Turnout: 68.5%

Source: Official figures, Stationery Office, Dublin.

The turmoil inside the Fianna Fáil Party after the 1992 contest in large measure reflected the challenge to its self-image as 'a national movement'. For many in Fianna Fáil, while other parties may represent sectional interests, only it is fully in tune with the broad mass of the Irish people, their aspirations and essential character. This sense of cultural centrality has made coalition with others an uncomfortable experience for many in the party. Some traditionalists and others, who wished to dislodge the current leader, reacted to the 1992 result by calling for a period in opposition. Out of government, it was argued, the party could assess how to regain its traditional hegemony by redefining its distinctive appeal, highlighting the mutual incompatibility of its opponents and improving its organisation.

Despite its internal debate Fianna Fáil had rarely enjoyed 50 per cent of the vote in general elections; 45 per cent was its average, and it had been favoured in terms of seats by the districting arrangements. A non-partisan commission now draws the constituency map and Fianna Fáil's slight advantage has gone. In 1992 it received its lowest percentage of seats in the Dáil. The party is still the largest in the Republic but it faces important problems of adjustment to its new role as 'another competitor' rather than 'presumed leader'. As a result of Fianna Fáil's performance, it is safe to assume that coalition is a permanent feature of the Republic's political landscape.

Fine Gael is generally categorised as a party of the right. In the 1960s, however, it adopted a distinctly left-of-centre programme with an emphasis on social justice and redistribution of wealth. During the recession of the 1980s fiscal rectitude became a more central part of the party's policy stance as Fine Gael positioned itself more clearly on the right. The coalition government between Fine Gael and Labour ended on a budgetary issue in 1987. Although social democrats are still an element within the party, Fine Gael is predominantly right wing. Nevertheless, in 1992 Fine Gael did benefit from its old ties with Labour at the vote transfer stage. However, the Fine Gael performance was its worst since 1948 in terms of votes and since 1957 in seats.

When a strong left-wing candidate was not available, Labour voters gave their lower preferences to Fine Gael. As a result, Fine Gael's disappointing 24.5 per cent of the first preference vote translated to 27 per cent of Dáil seats. There was also a close relationship between Fine Gael and the PDs in the 'transfer market'. The PDs adopted a strategic approach to the election and ran in selected constituencies only. Their share of the vote was 9.7 per cent in the constituencies in which they ran.

The election of 1992 was followed by a lengthy period of discussion between the parties on the formation of a new government. Eventually, on 12 January 1993, Fianna Fáil and Labour joined forces to provide an administration on the basis of an agreed programme (see below). The opposition parties, faced with a government majority of 34, moved very tentatively towards co-operation on strategy on the business of the Dáil.

Summary of the Fianna Fáil/Labour 'agreed programme' for government 1993

- Creation of 30,000 new jobs a year
- Improved tax relief for mortgage holders
- Reduced hospital waiting lists
- New local authority housing starts
- Reduced pupil/teacher ratio
- Radical measures to fight crime
- A light rail system for Dublin
- Creation of a state bank
- Establish Department of Enterprise and Employment
- Establish Department of Tourism and Foreign Trade
- May Day as public holiday
- Family law reform

In terms of the party system, the 1992 election may well prove a watershed. The opportunity is presented to Fine Gael to halt the decline in its fortunes by dominating the opposition to the new left-of-centre government. Its distinctively right-wing stance may help it position itself to advantage as the only credible alternative to Fianna Fáil. During the life of the previous government, Fine Gael was often overshadowed in the Dáil by the smaller Labour Party. In the 1992 election, it received 19.6 per cent of the middle-class vote in Dublin while Labour gained 26 per cent and Fianna Fáil 33.3 per cent. Clearly, the major opposition right-wing party could hope to increase this level of support if voting in the Republic is being determined increasingly by social and economic divisions of interest.

For Fianna Fáil, there is a major irony that they still lead the government after being so heavily defeated at the election. Several leading members have urged the party to become more self-consciously left wing. They stress the party's radical credentials and the level of its support in working-class Dublin constituencies, 32.4 per cent, 6.2 per cent more than Labour even in its *annus mirabilis*. Fianna Fáil is, however, still outstandingly the major party of the rural constituencies, where it picks up 42.8 per cent of the vote. In particular, its support is strongest in the poorer and most rural constituencies of the west of Ireland. The party must, therefore, seek to halt the swing away from it in Dublin, where it was almost 8 per cent, while retaining its attractiveness in rural Ireland.

Labour, supporting Fianna Fáil in government for the first time since 1932, must hope that its new electoral backing can be converted from an anti-incumbency protest to a genuine basis for growth. Its long-term aim must be to replace one of the two larger rivals and offer itself as a credible alternative major government party.

Changes in the party systems

The recent elections examined above do not confirm the prospects for change in either of the party systems in Ireland, although the Republic's are more promising. The cleavages that are expressed by the parties appear very persistent. Four possible reasons may be advanced for what Lipset and Rokkan call the 'freezing' of party systems, which can be characterised as:

- relevance;
- renewal;
- rules;
- reinforcement.

Relevance

Cleavages in society do not easily lose their relevance because they are based on salient and pressing issues. The link between unionism, Protestantism and well-being seem just as relevant to day-to-day life for many people in Northern Ireland as they did in former decades. While farmers in Antrim may have significantly different interests in public expenditure from those of shipyard workers in the Shankill, these differences are not as persuasive as their shared benefit in the safeguarding of partition. Similarly, the nationalist populism of Fianna Fáil is reassuring to those in the Republic who view with suspicion any sign of weakness on the 'national issue'. This appeal may seem to them to have greater strength than short-term misgivings about interest rates or employment levels.

Renewal

Once established, political parties have an interest in renewing the lines of cleavage by expressing their appeal in terms which already find popular resonance. The electorate of the 1920s and 1930s expanded rapidly as the franchise was widened. No new groups of people, other than 18–21 year olds, have joined since, so it is more difficult to attract voters by appeals to new alignments than to reinforce the existing lines of division. Ireland is not alone in having its party systems 'frozen' in a pattern reflecting cleavages which were first of political relevance several

decades ago. Nevertheless, Northern Ireland is extreme, in European terms, in the insularity of electoral competition within the two major communities.

Rules

The larger established parties effectively set the rules by which elections are conducted. It is difficult to alter the voting system, the funding mechanisms or administrative conventions of the state. Fianna Fáil twice failed to secure a constitutional change to alter the STV system of proportional representation, which they blamed for frequent government by coalition. The unionists abandoned STV in the 1920s to help ensure their subsequent control of the Stormont legislature. Its re-introduction for local and European elections under UK pressure was, in contrast, aimed at securing nationalist representation. It is unlikely that significant changes in the rules will occur in the near future in either Irish jurisdiction.

Reinforcement

The political parties that make up a party system are themselves important social organisations. Their existence often gives meaning to their supporters' private lives through meetings, social clubs and associated organisations. In Ireland, Fianna Fáil and the unionist parties are often the central part of a social network of overlapping memberships, which include church-related clubs and community organisations. Such networks, reinforced by the long experience of being in government, can give members and supporters a greater sense of belonging than may be implied by the instrumental decision to vote in a particular way.

These four factors of relevance, renewal, rules and reinforcement may help explain the stability of the Irish party systems. There are, however, new parties formed as well as older parties that decline. If Ireland's party systems are to change significantly, therefore, four possible causes might be isolated:

- discontinuities in society;
- demography;
- decline in relevance;
- disillusionment.

Discontinuities

The party systems in Ireland reflect the turbulent and dramatic effects of political and military events in the earlier parts of this century. Such dramatic discontinuities in a state's political life as a civil war or independence can threaten all existing institutions and often produce new ones, including political parties.

Since 1969, nearly 3,100 people have been killed in political violence in Northern Ireland and many more injured. This level of violence is sustained, in part, by the profound nature of the antagonism which existed between the two communities under the Stormont regime. This tension still has not dissipated despite major policy changes under subsequent administrations. The 'troubles' followed a period of civil unrest during which the nationalist community sought redress for serious and prolonged grievances. Many loyalists interpreted these demands as an attack on the viability and continuity of 'their' state. It is not surprising that both the DUP and SDLP were formed in this period, one as a radicalised splinter group of unionism, and the other a consolidation and reformulation of nationalism. A similar impact could be expected in the event of major constitutional or economic discontinuities.

Demography

Although popular media coverage of politics encourages a focus on electoral change as a result of contemporary events, colourful candidates and clever campaigns, most people always vote for the same party. This level of loyalty can still bring about change, however, if there is a decline or increase in the numerical strength of those social groups to which different parties appeal. The decline in the population of the rural west of Ireland or increase in the proportion of Catholics in Northern Ireland can be seen as impacting already on party fortunes. If such changes and similar demographic shifts became sufficiently large, they could seriously affect the party system.

Decline

The demographic changes that can influence the party system may well be related to another process, namely a decline in the sense of identification between a party and a particular social group. This sort of decline in relevance is the development most often cited as a possible cause for change in Ireland. Party identification, the idea that voters develop a bond to a particular party rather than choose it for instrumental reasons of self-interest, is a popular concept among Irish political analysts.

It is hard to find evidence to refute the power of traditional loyalties but it is possible that assessments of policy may be becoming more important. Certainly, government popularity is linked to economic policy performance in the Republic. Collectively, the electorate in the Republic has become less predictable in its decisions as the outcome of the 1992 election and the success of the new small parties make clear. Survey evidence shows that the young and urban voters are more likely to support new parties than the elderly, rural and small farm voters. Decline in relevance may, therefore, become a problem for Fianna Fáil and Fine Gael. In Northern Ireland, new parties, such as the Conservatives, are also seeking to exploit what they see as the declining relevance of the traditional cleavage.

Disillusionment

The decline in relevance of traditional cleavages to politics may be reinforced by a disillusion with current social structures generally. There is little evidence in Ireland that voters are disillusioned with political parties altogether. Individual politicians or even parties may be the subject of cynical comments but the political system still retains the confidence of the electorate of the Republic. In Northern Ireland, despite the residual support for the extra-constitutional violence of paramilitary groups, participation in elections and respect for the political process remains high. What evidence from elsewhere in Western Europe suggests is that, in the long term, some of the distinctiveness of class, religious and regional divisions may be declining. New so-called 'post materialist' issues centring on the concerns of post-industrial societies, new political value systems, such as feminism and environmentalism, and the emergence of distinctive organisational forms may lay the basis of realigned party systems.

The evidence for significant post-materialist influence on the party systems in Ireland is slight, though existing parties may eventually incorporate many such new ideas. In some other European states the stability of their party systems has been seriously challenged by the end of the Cold War, as well as by post-materialism. The weakening of the United States' economic strength, the reduction of its military commitment in Europe and the turmoil in Eastern Europe further undermined the post-war stability of politics in the West. Ireland can no longer insulate itself from the influence of such changes but the existing major cleavages on the island are likely to remain the dominant contingencies for some time to come.

Notes

1 On 15 November 1985 the British and Irish governments signed an agreement under which the Dublin authorities would be consulted on Northern Ireland affairs. The boost to the

confidence of moderate Catholic opinion which the signing of the Anglo-Irish Agreement represented was considerable. After over 60 years of frustration and limited recognition of the nationalist tradition, the unionist veto on progress had been removed. For Protestants the shock and dismay was profound and their anger led to street protests, strikes and civil disobedience. The two governments, however, remain committed to this internationally recognised treaty.

The agreement established an Intergovernmental Conference in which the Irish government would put forward views and proposals concerning stated aspects of Northern Ireland affairs and in which determined efforts would be made to resolve any differences between the two governments. The involvement of Dublin angered unionists but the Irish government's recognition of the status of Northern Ireland within the UK also upset diehard nationalist opinion. The agreement raised many expectations among Catholics that historic and recent grievances would be addressed.

2   Progress towards the resolution of many of the political problems of Northern Ireland has been slow, especially in the area of the administration of justice. Nevertheless, since the Anglo-Irish Agreement, the Protestant community has searched more earnestly for a compromise that would satisfy Catholics while defending their own interests. After much political manoeuvring, talks about the future government of Northern Ireland began in April 1991, involving the UK and Irish governments and those political parties in Northern Ireland which reject violence. Although a great many hopes for peace rested on the outcome, the talks ended in July without a settlement.

The public reaction to the politicians' failure to make headway was adverse. Peter Brooke, the Secretary of State, invited the parties to try again and on 9 March 1992 there was a four-hour meeting between the Secretary of State and the leaders of the four main 'constitutional' parties. Peter Brooke described this encounter as 'the first plenary meeting of the first strand of new political talks'. The participants agreed to renew dialogue after an Intergovernmental Conference to be held after the general election. These talks resumed under Mr Brooke's successor as Secretary of State, Sir Patrick Mayhew, and in early July 1992 he was able to announce further progress when it was agreed to move to the second strand of the process, involving the Irish and British governments as well as the parties.

Reference

Lipset, S. M., and Rokkan, S. (eds.) (1967), *Party Systems and Voter Alignments*, The Free Press, New York.

2 *Dennis Kennedy*

Constitutional change in the 1990s

A dictionary definition of a constitution is 'the system or body of fundamental principles according to which a nation, state or body politic is constituted and governed'. This can be a formal written document, as in the Republic of Ireland, or an accumulation of laws, customs and traditional practices as in the United Kingdom, or a combination of both. Not all constitutional rules or matters are necessarily included in a written constitution.

A constitution lays down rules for the principal organs of the state and government – how government is carried on, how the legislature works, and so forth. It is also concerned with the rights of the individual, and perhaps with public morality and other issues such as the rights of labour, or with a country's basic policy in international affairs.

Where there is a formal written constitution, there is also a formal procedure for altering it, usually of a fairly formidable nature, often involving a referendum of the population. The very existence of a written constitution, unless it is no more than a statement of principles, tends to imply an assumption that change is to be resisted, or at least possible only in very special circumstances.

As a legal document, however, a written constitution is open to interpretation by the courts, and in several countries it has been seen that legal interpretations by the appropriate judicial authority can mean a flexibility that was hitherto unsuspected, and a rate of change that was certainly not contemplated. This has happened, for instance, in the United States and Japan, as well as in the Republic of Ireland.

Where there is no written constitution, and where indeed there is usually no formal distinction between a 'constitutional' law and any other law, change is both much simpler and more frequent. All that is required is another law through the normal legislative process, and the constitutional significance of an alteration in the law may not be apparent at the time of change.

In the island of Ireland both types of constitution have existed since 1922, in that the south has, since independence, had a formal written constitution (from 1922 to 1937 the Free State of Ireland Constitution, and from 1937 onwards, the Constitution of Ireland), while the United Kingdom is the classic example of a state without one. Within the United Kingdom, however, the position of Northern Ireland has had to be defined by key pieces of legislation that are clearly 'constitutional' in nature, in that they define the position of Northern Ireland within the United Kingdom. This legislation lays down special provisions for the administration of Northern Ireland, and for the passing of legislation directly relevant to it.

A third type of constitutional instrument is also present in the island of Ireland – the international treaty. In 1921 the Anglo-Irish Treaty laid down many of the parameters within which the Irish framers of the Free State constitution of 1922 had to work. In 1985, the Anglo-Irish Agreement outlined in sketch form the type of constitutional arrangements for Northern Ireland which were considered possible in the long run. It instituted, in the short term, new arrangements for the governing of Northern Ireland which might loosely be regarded as constitutional.

Other international treaties also impact on constitutional arrangements within both parts of the island – the Treaties of Accession signed before the UK and Ireland joined the European Community in 1973 for example, and subsequent EC treaties such as the Single European Act and the European Union Treaty agreed in Maastricht in 1991.

In the case of the Republic, all these have required
formal amendment to the Constitution, including approval
by referendum. Within the United Kingdom, ratification by
Parliament has been all that is required. These changes
have been brought about by outside circumstances such as
membership of the European Community. These pressures
will continue and may well mean more and perhaps radical
constitutional changes in the 1990s. Basil Chubb has described
the potential impact on the rights of Irish citizens of the
European Community Treaties and their interpretation by the
European Court of Justice as 'immense'.[1]

Yet more intense pressure for constitutional re-arrangement
on both sides of the border will most likely stem from
the situation in Northern Ireland. This chapter will examine
possible constitutional changes in both jurisdictions over the
next decade. In this sense 'constitutional change' does not
necessarily have the meaning popularly assumed in discussion
of Northern Ireland, that is, alteration in the relationship of
Northern Ireland with the Republic of Ireland, though that is
not excluded.

Northern Ireland came into existence as a result of the
Government of Ireland Act of 1920. It was governed essentially
under the terms broadly laid down in that Act until 1972, that
is with its own regional government and Parliament in charge
of a range of matters devolved to them from London. That
situation continued from the creation of Northern Ireland in
1921 until the upheaval and violence following the civil rights
agitation of the late 1960s forced the government in London
to intervene directly and suspend the Stormont Parliament and
government.

The Northern Ireland (Temporary Provision) Act of 1972
prorogued Stormont and introduced direct rule from London,
with a Secretary of State for Northern Ireland responsible,
within the British Cabinet, for the administration of the area.
The Northern Ireland Constitution Act of 1973 allowed for
the brief period of devolution under a power-sharing executive
and Assembly in 1974. Direct rule was re-established in

mid-1974 under the Northern Ireland Act of that year, and has continued ever since. Another Northern Ireland Act in 1982 did offer a measure of devolution to the new Assembly elected that year, if sufficiently broad cross-community support for it could be found, which it never was. In addition, the Anglo-Irish Agreement of 1985 set up a London-Dublin Intergovernmental Conference to deal with specified policy areas within Northern Ireland – political matters, security and related matters, and legal matters, including the administration of justice. In these areas the Republic's government was given the right to put forward 'views and proposals', and both sides undertook to make 'determined efforts' to reach agreement on these.

Though the arrangements for governing Northern Ireland have remained largely unchanged for two decades (with the more recent addition of the Anglo-Irish Agreement dimension), they have been essentially temporary. They have been based on the expectation that there will be a return to devolution – to some arrangement under which an elected assembly in Northern Ireland, with an executive answerable to it, will take on responsibility for a wide range of policy areas. This expectation has been formally endorsed by the British government in the Anglo-Irish Agreement and supported by the Republic's government.

Further pressure for devolution arises from the unsatisfactory nature of direct rule. Under it the elected representatives of Northern Ireland – that is the seventeen Members of Parliament returned to Westminster – play almost no role in its governing. Not only are they all outside the political mainstream of Westminster, and therefore never likely to be part either of government or of official opposition, they have scant opportunity to influence Northern Ireland legislation, most of which is handled in the form of Orders in Council. These Orders, though they must be approved by the House of Commons, cannot be amended, and are, in general, little debated. Similarly, there is no Parliamentary time or scope at Westminster for routine scrutiny of all aspects of policy and administration as it affects Northern Ireland. This situation is made worse by the fact that district councils – the only publicly elected bodies in Northern Ireland – have very limited areas of responsibility.[2]

There is, therefore, steadily mounting pressure, both from government and from other sectors, for constitutional reforms which will restore a measure of responsibility for the affairs of Northern Ireland to representatives democratically elected by its inhabitants. This pressure can only be increased as the debate on devolution for other parts of the United Kingdom, notably Scotland, gains strength once more. Repeated opinion polls in Northern Ireland have shown clear majority support for devolution which must, in the words of the Anglo-Irish Agreement, 'secure widespread acceptance throughout the community' and 'can be achieved only with the co-operation of constitutional representatives within Northern Ireland of both traditions there'. Those traditions are defined in the Agreement and in repeated government statements as unionist and nationalist, that is 'those who wish for no change in the present status of Northern Ireland' and 'those who aspire to a sovereign united Ireland'.

It would seem clear that any form of devolution granted to Northern Ireland in the foreseeable future will not only have to be acceptable to both communities, but will actually have to include representatives of those two communities in any executive or government created under devolution. It remains an open question whether: (a) this is achieved by a mechanism similar to that of the NI Constitution Act 1973, whereby the Secretary of State played a central role and was essentially the judge of the cross-community nature of any possible executive, and if it was 'likely to be widely accepted throughout the community'; or (b) whether there is explicit requirement for 'the two traditions' to be represented.

An objection to both methods is that they institutionalise the two 'traditions', setting up a sort of apartheid, and offering little hope of practical politics evolving across the sectarian divide. Some voices have favoured an alternative route, suggesting a devolved executive should require the support of a significant, and specified, majority in any elected assembly, making rule by one community alone impossible. Just such a provision was written into the Northern Ireland Act 1982. The Assembly created under that Act was given the power to propose a Northern Ireland executive with devolved powers if it had the support of at least 70 per cent of its members. This would, in practice, mean support from both communities, but would stop short of freezing politics in a sectarian mould. It would leave the way more open for the evolution of new political groups drawing support from both sides.

The degree of devolution, the identifying of the specific policy areas to be devolved to a Northern Ireland Assembly and Executive, would also be a key issue. Here what happens in Scotland and the rest of the UK will be important. There will be, however, specially sensitive areas in Northern Ireland, most notably in security. Devolution could be progressive, with policy areas being devolved as agreement on them is reached among the parties in Northern Ireland.

Devolution in the generally accepted sense of a regional assembly and executive may not be the only way forward. There have been proposals for more limited forms, for instance for an elected assembly which would monitor the activities of 'direct rule' ministers through a series of specialist committees, as happened to a limited extent in the 1982–86 assembly. The difficulty of reaching cross-community agreement on full devolution, coupled with the increasingly obvious shortcomings of direct rule – 'an almost complete absence of representative participation and accountability' as one writer has put it – keeps open the possibility of such compromise measures.[3]

The task of reaching agreement inside Northern Ireland on constitutional change is greatly complicated by the now well-established need to incorporate some 'Irish dimension'. In the context of the current troubles this first appeared in modest form in the 1973 Northern Ireland Constitution Act, which gave a Northern Ireland executive the power to consult directly with the authorities in the Republic, and to enter into agreements on matters within its competence. (Under the old Stormont system contact with Dublin was generally regarded as a United Kingdom matter, handled between London and Dublin.) Considerable enlargement of this dimension was planned before the 1974 power-sharing executive came into being through the Sunningdale Agreement, which foresaw a Council of Ireland, made up of a Council of Ministers from Belfast and Dublin, and a Consultative Assembly of elected representatives from North and South. The collapse of the executive meant this dimension was never realised. However, the British-Irish Intergovernmental Council established between London and Dublin in 1981, and expanded under the Anglo-Irish Agreement, has effectively brought it into being in the broader British-Irish context, without devolution in Northern Ireland, and despite unionist rejection of the new institutions.

Incorporating an Irish dimension acceptable to a majority in Northern Ireland into any future arrangement for devolution will be among the most difficult challenges. This will be particularly so as it has become clear, notably during the round-table talks of 1992, that nationalist thinking is more and more looking towards joint British-Irish authority over Northern Ireland. The so-called European model proposal put forward by the SDLP in the course of 1992, with an executive commission for Northern Ireland, half of which would be elected and half appointed through nomination by Brussels, London and Dublin, was a rather complicated step in this direction, involving as it did a considerable dilution of British authority over Northern Ireland through the incorporation of roles for the Republic and the European Community.[4]

This SDLP proposal was generally seen as impractical; European Commission involvement was ruled out by the Commission President Jacques Delors on a visit to Belfast in November 1992.[5] Nevertheless it did indicate the strength of nationalist feeling that a major constitutional re-arrangement, as distinct from new mechanisms within the present framework, is needed.

While it is generally assumed that constitutional change in Northern Ireland can come about only when there is general agreement on it across the main political groups, this is not necessarily so. The imposition of the Anglo-Irish Agreement in 1985, when the majority community in Northern Ireland was not consulted in advance, and when it strenuously rejected the Agreement, has set a precedent for the Secretary of State to bring forward a major initiative without prior agreement, and to implement it without majority consent. The Agreement does decree that there can be no constitutional change in the status of Northern Ireland without approval of a majority there, but in the absence of a written constitution there can still be argument over what is, or is not, a change in constitutional status. The Agreement, while itself asserting it involved no such change, did implement far-reaching innovations which were, arguably, of a constitutional nature.

In the face of continued failure to reach agreement through all-party talks there will be pressure, from Dublin and the nationalist side generally, to follow this precedent and impose still more radical change on Northern Ireland while arguing that such change does not, technically, alter the constitutional status of the region. The constitutional guarantee to Northern Ireland contained in the Anglo-Irish agreement may be less precise than it sounds, as the two government signatories to the Agreement did not, and do not, agree on what that status is.

While devolution is the most favoured constitutional option, there is a growing body of support for continued direct rule from London, with improved arrangements for the handling of Northern Ireland business at Westminster. This remains a possibility, particularly if agreement among the parties in Northern Ireland proves to be impossible.

Another element in constitutional proposals in Northern Ireland in the 1990s will be the idea of a Bill of Rights. This has been proposed by various groups as a way of guaranteeing, through one comprehensive piece of legislation, fair treatment for all. A step in this direction was taken in the Constitution Act 1973, which set up the Standing Advisory Commission on Human Rights. This independent body has monitored the effectiveness of laws against discrimination, and has frequently taken a critical stance towards government. But until recently there has been no general agreement that a Bill of Rights for Northern Ireland is either necessary or desirable.

In the 1970s the Standing Advisory Commission itself conducted an intensive study into the question and produced a report in 1977. This concluded that while a substantial body of law already existed in Northern Ireland to protect various aspects of human rights, there was need for further protection. One of the ways in which this could be achieved was by the enactment of an enforceable Bill of Rights for the United Kingdom as a whole, and the best way of doing this would be to incorporate the European Convention on Human Rights into the domestic law of the UK. At the same time, the report said that in the event of a return to devolution, it would be desirable for legislation governing devolution to include 'a clear and enforceable Charter of Rights for Northern Ireland'. This could be more comprehensive than the European Convention and more tailored to the special needs of Northern Ireland.[6]

Advocates of a Bill of Rights for Northern Ireland, regardless of what happens in the UK as a whole, argue that the absence of such a legal protection for fundamental values in the past made easier the abuse of power by the political majority, government and officials. Others argue that a Bill of Rights, which must be general in nature, can offer no such blanket protection, and would simply raise expectations which could not be satisfied. The argument now, however, seems to be one of legal detail, not political principle.

Constitutional change in the Republic of Ireland in the 1990s will probably come in three areas – changes stemming from developments within the European Community, changes stemming from evolving public attitudes, such as a move to delete the clause prohibiting the enactment of divorce law, and changes related to the Northern Ireland question.

The year 1992 saw a constitutional amendment to take account of the European Community Treaty on European

Union agreed at Maastricht at the end of 1991. The government under Albert Reynolds has indicated its intention of looking again at another attempt to remove the prohibition of divorce. Further, the court injunction in February 1992 restraining a young girl from leaving the country to seek an abortion in England once again brought that aspect of the Constitution into sharp controversy. This court battle, known as the 'X Case', led to a triple referendum on abortion in November, which still left the question unresolved.

The Irish Constitution (Bunreacht na hEireann) dates from 1937 and has proved remarkably rigid, thanks partly to the procedure for amendment laid down in it, requiring approval for any change by public referendum. An initial settling-in period was fixed to allow early change by Parliament alone, but after two such amendments, the Constitution remained unaltered until 1972. In that year three amendments passed; one was essential to allow the Republic to enter the European Community, another lowered the voting age to 18 and the third removed the reference in Article 44 to the special position of the Catholic Church.

Since then further changes have been made, three of them essentially technical matters, and a fourth required by signature of the Single European Act 1986. Another change was the highly controversial addition of an anti-abortion (or 'pro-life') clause in 1983. In 1986, a move to delete the prohibition on divorce was defeated at referendum by 936,000 votes to 538,000. Three further amendments relating to abortion were voted on in 1992, all of them resulting from the need to take account of the verdict in the X Case. Two, relating to the right to travel and the right to information, were passed; the third, on the more substantive issue of abortion itself, was defeated. New legislation in the area is therefore necessary. The whole incident has illustrated the pitfalls of a written constitution going into detailed prohibitions and regulations which might, perhaps, be better left to legislation.

The Anglo-Irish Agreement, though clearly of great constitutional significance to the Irish Republic, did not require any change to the Constitution. The Supreme Court ruled that nothing in the Agreement conflicted with the existing Constitution, when this was alleged in a case brought before it.

There has as yet been no formal attempt to alter the most controversial clauses of the Constitution – those asserting what is called the 'territorial claim' to Northern Ireland. Article 2 states: 'The national territory consists of the whole island of Ireland, its islands and territorial seas'. Article 3 acknowledges that 'pending the re-unification of the national territory' laws enacted in Parliament in Dublin will apply only to the 26 counties. It does so, however, 'without prejudice to the right of the Parliament and Government established by this Constitution to exercise jurisdiction over the whole of that territory'.

As long ago as 1967 an all-party committee of senior Dáil politicians concluded that it was then appropriate to replace the assertion in Article 2, that the whole island was the national territory, with a proclamation 'by the Irish Nation': of its 'firm will that its territory be reunited in harmony and brotherly affection between all Irishmen'. By its references to 'the Irish Nation' and 'its territory' this wording retained by implication the claim to the North, but in much less provocative terms. It was, however, generally unacceptable to the political establishment. Since then, though individual politicians and groups have advocated prompt changes to Article 2, there has been no formal proposal to do so. Instead, governments in Dublin have adopted the posture that such changes can be considered only in the context of a general North-South negotiation on a new and presumably unified Ireland, or at least some sort of 'agreed' Ireland. Even the New Ireland Forum in 1984 saw no need to alter the Constitution or its territorial claims prior to the dawning of the New Ireland itself.

At the same time, the Constitution has not inhibited successive Irish governments signing Treaties with the government of the United Kingdom of Great Britain and Northern Ireland, nor formally recognising 'the status of Northern Ireland', as in the Sunningdale Agreement 1973, and, most notably, the

Anglo-Irish Agreement 1985. Article 1 of the Anglo-Irish Agreement states that 'The two governments affirm that any change in the status of Northern Ireland would only come about with the consent of a majority of the people in NI'.

As has been pointed out, the Agreement nowhere defined exactly what that status was, leaving the Irish Government free to maintain that the reference was to the status as enshrined in Articles 2 and 3 of the Constitution. Inaction over Articles 2 and 3 in the Republic was also encouraged, throughout the 1970s and 1980s, by the general view that they were a political declaration, not a formal territorial claim with legal effect. The judgement of the Supreme Court in the McGimpsey v. Ireland case (1990) has radically altered that. The Court ruled that the reintegration of the national territory referred to in Article 3 was 'a constitutional imperative', and that Article 2 was indeed a 'claim of legal right' over the whole island.[7]

The full implications of this judgement could be very significant indeed in the context of any revision of the Anglo-Irish Agreement, or its replacement. In the course of the 1992 all-party talks, Articles 2 and 3 emerged as a major issue, with Dublin's refusal to make any unilateral concession on them proving a major stumbling block. Criticism of the Irish Government's stance came not just from the Unionist parties, but also from Alliance and from other parties in the Republic. Pressure for change seems bound to increase in the 1990s, in contrast to the previous decade. There has been a widespread belief in the Republic over the past decade that progress was being made. In particular, the Anglo-Irish Agreement was thought to provide a framework for movement towards a solution. In those circumstances, there seemed no urgent need to consider changes in the Constitution, which would in any event have to be part of the negotiated settlement which, it was thought, was probable under the umbrella of the Agreement.

With Unionist rejection of the Agreement showing no signs of abatement, and with a steady increase in violence, there is growing need for a fresh look at the agreed London-Dublin

policy on Northern Ireland. Several commentators have pointed
to Articles 2 and 3 as providing encouragement to the IRA,
which can claim that it is pursuing an objective – re-unification
of the national territory – which is formally enshrined in the
Constitution. While this is clearly a highly theoretical point, it
is one more argument for change. It seems likely, therefore, that
Articles 2 and 3 will have a formal challenge sooner rather than
later. It might be as well to look at Article 4 at the same time,
as the designation of the name of the state as 'Ireland' could be
construed as a claim to the whole island of the same name.

The Irish government might be glad to look again at Article
4 for its own reasons. It is Article 4 which states that the name
of the country is Eire – that is what it says in the English text
of the Constitution. So the more conservative English papers
and many Unionists who use the term 'Eire' to the great and
manifest annoyance of Dublin are, in fact, constitutionally
correct. Article 4 also gives the English language alternative
of 'Ireland', but just as other Irish language terms such as
Taoiseach, Dáil and Seanad have entered into general English
usage, so it was no doubt the intention of the Constitution's
author in the 1930s, Eamon de Valera, that the country should
be called Eire.

At various times in recent years there have been suggestions
for changes in other clauses of the Constitution, usually in the
context of discussion of re-unification or relations with the
North. Garret FitzGerald, for instance, has said the article
dealing with the primacy of the Irish language should be
examined.[8] But there is evidence that the momentum for change
comes from the citizens of the Republic themselves. The strong,
but as yet minority support for the removal of the prohibition
on divorce has its roots in social concern in the Republic, not
in relation to Northern Ireland. The campaign in 1983 which
resulted in the inclusion of the anti-abortion amendment clearly
regarded the impact of such a move on the Northern question as
secondary, if not irrelevant. Such pressures, whether in a liberal
or a conservative direction, are likely to increase in the 1990s,
particularly in the context of a European single market, where

free movement of people is guaranteed, and where the freedom to provide services across internal EC boundaries will, in some instances, conflict with a desire to preserve the Catholic ethos of the 1930s which still permeates the Constitution.

All these are highly controversial matters, as – to a lesser extent – are some of the changes related to the European Community, for instance a perceived threat to the Republic's traditional neutrality. They raise the prospect of a succession of divisive and bitterly contested referendums, with no guarantee that the proposed changes will be made. In these circumstances the question of an entirely new constitution, less detailed and less restrictive, is bound to be raised in the course of the next decade, either to take account of a 'New Ireland' or, more likely, to try to make life in the present divided one less complicated and less dangerous.

Notes

1   Chubb, B. (1991), *The Politics of the Irish Constitution*, Institute of Public Administration, Dublin, p. 18.
2   For a concise account of direct rule see Flackes, W. D. and S. Elliott (1989), *Northern Ireland: A Political Directory*, Blackstaff, Belfast, p. 364.
3   Hadfield, B. (1992), *Politics and the Constitution in Northern Ireland*, Open University Press, Buckingham.
4   *Irish Times*, 13 May 1992.
5   *Irish Times*, 4 November 1992.
6   Standing Advisory Commission on Human Rights (1977), *The Protection of Human Rights by Law in Northern Ireland*, Cmnd 7009.
7   For a brief account of the McGimpsey case see Hadfield, *Politics and Constitution*, p. 176.
8   FitzGerald, G. (1972), *Towards a New Ireland*, Charles Knight, Dublin and London, p. 150.

Managing Europe

The Republic of Ireland and Northern Ireland joined the EC on the first of January 1973 as part of the first enlargement. The Republic is a full member state whereas Northern Ireland entered as a part of the United Kingdom. For the Republic, community membership represented the most important foreign policy decision taken since the Second World War. Accession to the EC involved joining a club of 'Nine' (now 'Twelve') states in a voluntary pooling or sharing of national sovereignty.

Signing up for an unknown destination

Inter-state relations in the EC are based on an independent legal order that creates rights and obligations for the member states, enterprises and citizens. Community law is federal in character in that its laws become part of the national legal systems. EC Regulations are directly applicable in the member states once they are passed by the Council of Ministers. Furthermore, the supremacy of Community law over national law in the event of conflict is an established principle of this federalist legal system. Individual citizens have recourse to the Court of Justice in Luxembourg if a member state is failing to meet its obligations under Community law.

The goal of the European Community goes beyond that of traditional international organisations. The Treaty of Rome spoke of 'ever closer union among the peoples of Europe'. By joining the EC, a state joins an evolving entity that is constantly changing. EC membership is much more than a once-off commitment to pooling sovereignty. The term 'union' is sufficiently vague and ambiguous to mean many different things to different interests. There has always been a tension in the Community between sovereignty and integration, between the continued existence of strong nation states in Western Europe and growing co-operative arrangements. The tension has usually been expressed in term of 'supranationalism' and 'intergovernmentalism'. 'Supranationalism' usually refers to institutions that are independent of the member states. 'Intergovernmentalism', on the other hand, connotes traditional inter-state diplomatic bargaining. Politics in the EC have always been a mixture of 'supranationalism' and 'inter-governmentalism'.

In 1985, the member states agreed to the first modification of the Treaty of Rome in the form of the Single European Act (SEA). This followed a period of considerable stagnation when the EC was largely irrelevant to the many problems confronting the recession-torn economies of Western Europe. The resurgence of integration in the mid-1980s owes much to what is known in popular parlance as the '1992 programme'. This was a serious attempt to abolish the remaining barriers to free economic exchange among the Community states. It involved an ambitious programme of legislation to abolish hidden barriers to trade, protectionism in the services sector and restrictive public procurement policies.

The Single European Act was seen as a necessary component of the 1992 programme because without institutional change many of the proposed laws would have languished in the Council of Ministers, where individual Ministers were prepared to veto proposed legislation. The Single European Act extended the use of qualified majority voting in the Council of Ministers. This means that in practice individual ministers can be outvoted in the Council but must implement the said law at national level in any case.

The apparent success of the Single European Act and the internal market programme in reviving the fortunes of the European Community led to renewed emphasis on the Community as a forum for problem solving in Western Europe. In 1989, the Community set its sights on an Economic and Monetary Union (EMU) with the publication of a report by the President of the Commission, Jacques Delors, on EMU. A common currency was seen as the 'jewel in the crown' of economic integration. Political union came to the fore with the collapse of communism in Eastern Europe, the ensuing unification of Germany and disintegration in the Soviet Union. Given the pace of change in international politics and in Europe, the Community emerged as the core regional organisation and anchor of stability for the continent as a whole. Membership of the EC became the primary goal of a number of EFTA states that had long shunned integration and for the countries of Eastern/Central Europe, 'rejoining Europe' meant accession to the EC.

Arising from the challenges of the new Europe, the member states began a second round of constitution building with two Intergovernmental Conferences on Political Union and Economic and Monetary Union. At the Maastricht European Council in December 1991, the member states agreed to the text of a treaty establishing a 'European Union'. The new Treaty establishes the policy agenda for the 1990s and represents an acceleration in the pace of European integration. The Treaty contains a commitment to the establishment of a common currency by the end of the 1990s and includes a chapter on a common foreign and security policy.

European integration is a mixture of politics and economics. Although the substance of much of the Community's activity is economic, there is an underlying political dynamic to European integration. Most areas of public policy, agriculture, trade, vocational training and economic management have an important EC dimension. States are no longer free to pursue independent policies in those areas that are dealt with in the EC treaties. Nor is the high politics of security and defence

immune from a European dimension. There is in Western
Europe a 'fourth level of government' operating above the
level of the state.

Managing integration

EC membership has direct consequences for a country's
political, administrative and judicial systems. There has been
an intermingling and intermeshing of the political and judicial
systems of the member states and the Community. European
integration is part of how the Western European states have
responded to the political and economic challenges of the
post-war world. Economic integration made the countries of
Western Europe more interdependent. Economic integration
tends to have both beneficial and damaging effects on economic
activity. Some sectors and regions benefited more than others.
For small, open, peripheral economies like those of the Republic
and Northern Ireland, economic integration poses immense
challenges of competitiveness. Yet there are few options, given
the nature of contemporary international economics and politics.
In or out of the Community, Ireland is not immune to the
increasing internationalisation of economic activity. Membership
of the EC provides both parts of Ireland with access to markets
and involvement in the core organisation in Western Europe,
if not in Europe as a whole. That said, all small states face
problems of how to manage the boundaries between themselves
and the outside world.

The pre-accession inheritance

Ireland's first application for Community membership, like the
United Kingdom application, was made in the early 1960s but
made no progress because General de Gaulle vetoed United
Kingdom membership. The motivation for the Irish application
was the result of a change in domestic economic policy. In 1958,

the Republic's Government opted for a policy of economic growth fuelled by investment from outside the country. In order to attract foreign capital, Ireland needed to accept the challenge of free trade and gain entry to a trading block. The lure of modernisation was a powerful motivation behind the decision to seek membership of the Community.

In 1972, following the negotiations on an Accession Treaty, the issue of membership was put to a referendum. There was an overwhelming vote in favour of joining 'Europe'; in a high poll of 71 per cent, 83 per cent voted in favour and 17 per cent against. The issue of membership did not lead to division in the Republic's political parties. The two main parties, Fianna Fáil and Fine Gael, advocated membership whereas the Labour party provided the parliamentary opposition. There was thus a high degree of consensus about membership among the Irish public and little of the reticence found in the United Kingdom and Denmark.

The referendum debate in the Republic provides a useful overview of the kinds of issues that were likely to dominate Ireland's EC politics. Economic considerations rather than political ones had centre stage. While opponents of membership opposed the loss of sovereignty that EC membership entailed, the proponents argued that for a small state the pooling or sharing of sovereignty was preferable to formal sovereignty that could not be exercised. The likely benefits from the Common Agricultural Policy, financial transfers from the social and regional funds and the possibility of new markets were all highlighted during the campaign. Neutrality was the only contentious political issue to emerge at the hustings. Its non-membership of NATO made the Republic an 'odd man out' in the Nine and later the Twelve. The Government at the time stressed the economic rather than the political character of European integration. Therefore although there was overwhelming support for membership, this was not necessarily support for political integration.

For Northern Ireland, the prospect of EC membership came at a time of intense political turbulence from 1969 onwards. The so-called 'troubles' served to downplay the issue of EC membership. In any event, the traditional separation of powers between Stormont and Whitehall meant that the latter negotiated the terms of membership on behalf of the entire United Kingdom. Therefore, although there were strong reservations about the possible adverse economic consequences of EC membership, the Stormont government left the negotiations to Whitehall. In 1972, Stormont itself was prorogued and Northern Ireland found itself under 'direct rule' from London. The political and security problems of Northern Ireland were far higher on the agenda than EC membership.

In Northern Ireland, the question of EC membership was put to a vote in 1975 after the then Labour government in London renegotiated the terms of British membership of the Community. This afforded Northern Ireland's political parties an opportunity to declare their views on European integration. There is a distinct party political cleavage on the issue. The unionists (UUP and DUP) are both essentially hostile to the EC whereas the SDLP and the Alliance are pro-European in ethos. Sinn Féin oppose European integration, seeing it as a dilution of Irish sovereignty and nationalism.

Inevitably, the issue of European integration became embroiled in the deep-rooted conflict about Northern Ireland's consti- tutional position. The SDLP, particularly under the leadership of John Hume, saw European integration as a means of lessening the salience of the Irish border and of promoting Irish unity under the guise of European unity. A Europe of 'the regions' is a related theme in SDLP thinking. For unionists, European integration became the Trojan horse that could have adverse consequences for their position within the United Kingdom. The Christian democratic origins of the EC raised the spectre of 'Rome Rule'. Notwithstanding Unionist fears about European integration, the referendum was carried by a narrow majority in Northern Ireland. Fifty-two per cent of those who voted supported EC membership in a low poll of forty-seven per cent.[1]

Interests and preoccupations

An economic community

Although there are differences among the political parties in Northern Ireland and the Republic concerning European integration, the island's socio-economic position in the EC greatly influences the policies pursued in Brussels. Both parts of Ireland have lower levels of economic well-being than the central heartland of the EC. Per capita income is less than 75 per cent of the EC average in the Republic and just 89 per cent in Northern Ireland. Using a synthetic index of regional disparity devised by the European Commission, the Republic of Ireland is the sixth weakest region in the Community and Northern Ireland is ranked the thirty-third weakest.[2] The difference between the Republic and Northern Ireland is explained by the significant transfer of resources from the United Kingdom budget to Northern Ireland. High unemployment is a feature of life in both economies. Agriculture plays an important part in the island's economy.

A heavy reliance on external trade, a large agricultural sector and peripherality shape the response to EC developments. There is greater emphasis placed on the economic than the political aspects of integration. It was not until the successful Crotty challenge to the constitutionality of the Single European Act in 1987 that the political nature of the Community received sustained attention in the Republic. A constant theme in Ireland's European policy is that political integration must develop in tandem with economic integration. Put simply, the Republic will accept political integration provided that the benefits of economic integration are evenly distributed and extended to all regions of the EC. This approach has been summed up as 'conditionally integrationist' by a former Minister of State for European Affairs, Mrs Máire Geoghegan-Quinn.

For the Republic, the protection of the fundamental principles of the Common Agricultural Policy, notably price support, intervention and protection *vis-à-vis* low cost third country producers, assumes high priority in the management of

Community politics. Reluctantly, the country's political leaders have had to face up to the need for reform in the CAP. Wine lakes, butter and beef mountains highlight the need for change. Pressure on the Community budget and demands by the United States in the GATT negotiations for fundamental reform of the CAP have greatly altered the policy environment of agricultural policies. In any event, the CAP, although it increased farm prices and farm incomes for some periods since accession, did not solve the problems of low farm incomes for many Irish farmers. Nor did it lead to a strengthening of the food sector, which would have added value to Irish farm production. For Northern Ireland, the UK government's opposition to the fundamentals of the CAP, and its sustained assault on the policy since accession, have not always been in its interests. Paradoxically, concessions on side-payments negotiated by the Dublin civil servants on agricultural matters have been extended to Northern Ireland.

The politics of redistribution loom large in the minds of politicians and officials on both sides of the border. The Dublin government has always been an advocate of the need for cohesion and solidarity in the Community. During the negotiations on the Single Act in 1985, the Republic, together with the other poorer parts of the EC, used the negotiating opportunity to press for a strengthening of redistributive policies. A new treaty chapter on 'economic and social cohesion' resulted from the negotiations. This was followed in 1988 by the Delors plan of budgetary reform. The doubling of the resources of the structural funds (social fund, regional fund and agricultural fund) in the run up to 1992 was seen as an essential part of market liberalisation. Fear that a barrier-free Europe would have adverse consequences for the less developed parts of the EC was the main reason behind the 1988 reform of the structural funds. Not only was there an increase in the resources of the funds but the manner of their distribution was significantly changed. Instead of a plethora of individual project submissions, financial support was dependent on the submission of a development plan to Brussels setting out a coherent framework for development. The Commission formulated its own Community Support

Framework in response to the plan. The reform of the funds
sought to give the Commission a greater say over the use to
which its monies were put and to enable it to establish links
with regional and local government within the member states.
This led to considerable contention in the Republic because of
the centralised nature of government and the absence of local
authority autonomy. The government was forced to establish
regional development committees to draft plans for structural
fund monies. Although the exercise was largely symbolic, their
continued existence as monitoring committees may, in the longer
term, contribute to the establishment of a regional tier of
government in the Republic. Northern Ireland was included
as an Objective One area following the reform of the funds.
Although its per capita income was above the threshold of 75
per cent of the Community average, the particular circumstances
of the region made it an exception.

The costs of German unification and the need to aid the
transition to democracy and to market economies in the former
Eastern bloc have added a new dimension to the politics of
redistribution in Europe. Neither the Commission nor the
governments representing the richer states wanted to discuss
'cohesion' or Community solidarity in the Conferences on
Political Union and EMU. This was extraordinary given the
need within an EMU to have some capacity for macro-economic
management and some capacity to respond to economic shocks.
Sustained diplomatic pressure from Spain, Ireland, Portugal and
Greece ensured that 'cohesion' became an agenda item. Spain
wanted a fundamental reform of the EC budget to include some
form of automatic transfer from the richer to the poorer parts of
the Community. Although this was not forthcoming, there was
agreement at Maastricht to the establishment of a new 'cohesion
fund'. This fund will finance environmental and transport
measures.

Under the terms of the protocol on economic and social
cohesion appended to the Treaty of Maastricht, Northern
Ireland is excluded from this fund because it specifically refers
to 'member states', not regions. Northern Ireland will, however,

be eligible for support from the structural funds which will receive additional monies in the Delors II package agreed at the Edinburgh European Council in 1992. There is also the prospect of financial transfers from the cohesion fund established by the agreement between the EC and EFTA on a European Economic Area. The Agreement refers to the 'whole island of Ireland'.

Although 'solidarity' among the member states is an accepted goal in the EC, there is somewhat of a gap between the rhetoric and reality. The EC budget and the structural funds are too small and distributed in too rigid a manner to have a sizeable impact on economic disparities. Economic theory offers very little in terms of clearcut prescription for overcoming regional disparities and the economic impact of peripherality. Moreover, the EC is not sufficiently developed as a political system to allow for major transfers across regions.

The emphasis in Ireland's policy on budgetary transfers, although understandable, leads to a narrow cost benefit approach to the EC. The lure of Brussels grants can distort planning and budgeting at national level as administrators seek a maximum return from the EC's structural funds. More attention is paid to actually managing the politics of grantsmanship than to the economic or development process the grants are supposed to assist. The Brussels connection can reinforce a psychological environment of dependency and serve to obscure the need for sound economic management at national level. Doubtless, the questions of cohesion and economic divergence will continue to loom large for both parts of Ireland as the EC expands its membership and deepens the level of integration.

High politics

The Republic's military neutrality has proved compatible with European integration since accession because of the restricted scope of foreign policy co-operation in the EC and the stability of the continent's security system until the revolutions of 1989. NATO's predominance as the forum for Western Europe's defence allowed the EC to develop as a 'civilian power'. Security, in the broadest sense of the term, began to impinge on the Community's agenda in the 1980s. The Single European Act in 1986 included the 'political and economic' aspects of security as part of the remit of European Political Co-operation. The consequence of this for Irish neutrality and independence in foreign policy was one of the main themes in the 1987 referendum on the Single European Act.

The Intergovernmental Conference on Political Union addressed the issue of a common foreign and security policy for the EC. The ensuing agreement in the Treaty of Maastricht to new provisions in this field marks a qualitative change in the Community's goals in the international arena. The Treaty uses the term 'security' in its broadest sense without qualification. Furthermore, the Treaty makes provision for the possibility of majority voting on joint actions among the member states in the sphere of foreign policy. The Treaty also contains a commitment to discuss a common defence policy in 1996 and the development of a European defence capability.

Thus, while the Treaty of Maastricht does not signify the abandonment of the Republic's traditional policy, it does raise the possibility of a mutual defence pact or some sort of alliance commitment in the future. The development of security politics within the Community depends very much on the evolution of the NATO Alliance. Most EC states remain committed to NATO as Western Europe's defence organisation, while accepting that there is a need for a Western European defence identity. The Western European Union provides the basis for a European defence dimension in the immediate future. The management of the politics of security is likely to be one of the most sensitive for Ireland in the 1990s.

Local politics

Membership of the EC by both the UK and the Republic has had an impact on the conduct of their relations concerning Northern Ireland and on internal politics there. The placing of

Anglo-Irish relations in the multilateral setting of the EC helped to create an atmosphere of trust between the two governments. Meetings between the heads of both governments at the margins of European Councils facilitated bilateral relations. The Milan Summit in 1985 not only relaunched European integration, but also allowed for some sensitive talks on the Anglo-Irish Agreement to take place. In many ways, the Agreement itself is modelled on the Community's policy style, with its emphasis on co-operative arrangements and a continuing cycle of meetings.

Relations among the political parties in Northern Ireland are affected by European integration. Community institutions provide an arena for influence and are the source of some material benefits. From the outset the unionists were determined to see that there would be no political discussion of Northern Ireland within the institutions of the EC. The SDLP, for its part, used the political access gained by a seat in the European Parliament to raise Northern Ireland on the Community's agenda. John Hume has sought to ensure that the political nature of the conflict in Northern Ireland would not be neglected. After painstaking lobbying, the Political Affairs Committee of the European Parliament initiated the Haagerup report on Northern Ireland in 1984. The unionists were deeply resentful about the report, seeing it as unwarranted interference in the affairs of Northern Ireland and confirming their suspicions about European integration.

Despite constitutional differences of view, Northern Ireland's MEPs have found common cause in the Parliament on economic issues. After direct elections in 1979, Northern Ireland's three MEPs, Ian Paisley, John Hume and John Taylor, banded together to promote Northern Ireland as a region needing special treatment. As a consequence of this, one of the Community's first so-called Integrated Development Operations was set up in Belfast. As noted above, Northern Ireland has remained a priority region for EC development funds although its per capita income level is higher than the agreed cut-off point. European integration has provided opportunities for agreement among Northern Ireland political parties provided it does not impinge on constitutional politics.

Managing the policy process

The EC adds an additional layer of government to politics. Each member state or region in the Community attempts to ensure that its interests are protected in EC policy making. However, not all states or regions carry equal weight. The Republic of Ireland is a small member state with just over three million people on the periphery of the Community. Northern Ireland is a region within one of the Community's larger member states. All major policy and institutional developments in the Community must be promoted by at least two of the larger states. Small states tend to focus on a limited range of areas that impinge directly on their interests. Coalition-building with like-minded states is an important component of the policy process.

The Republic's full membership of the Community gives it direct access to the EC's policy process and institutions. Irish ministers sit at the Council of Ministers' table as equals. The Taoiseach is a member of the European Council, the highest level in the Community's decision-making process. The Republic has one Commissioner and a judge at the Court of Justice. In contrast, the only direct representation Northern Ireland has is its three MEPs in the European Parliament. The Republic has 15 MEPs, giving the island 18 MEPs out of a total of 518.

The Republic's full membership of the EC extends to active participation in the multitude of committees under the aegis of the Council and the Commission. The management of the Brussels policy process or the 'fourth level of government' poses a considerable strain on the limited administrative resources of the state, especially during the rotating Presidency when, for six months, the Republic must chair all EC meetings and manage the agenda. The Presidency is, however, very important for the small states because it affords them an opportunity to be at the centre of EC business. An effective Presidency can enhance a country's standing and may contribute a store of diplomatic goodwill for future bargaining.

Involvement in the intensity of EC policy-making has impinged greatly on the lives of ministers and civil servants. There has been a 'Europeanisation' of government in the Republic. Many ministers, notably those in Foreign Affairs, Finance, Agriculture, and Industry and Commerce meet their counterparts in other countries with considerable regularity. Civil servants spend a considerable amount of time flying between Brussels and Dublin, working with their counterparts in other member states in an effort to hammer out agreements on the many issues that form part of the Community's policy agenda. Procedures are needed in Dublin to ensure that the policy line adopted in Brussels is reasonably coherent. Administrative arrangements include a system of inter-departmental co-ordination feeding into what is known as the European Communities Committee. There are also Cabinet sub-committees on major EC developments.

In contrast to the Republic, Northern Ireland does not have any direct involvement in the Community's policy process apart from three representatives in the Parliament. It has been argued that Northern Ireland is disadvantaged in the EC because its interests can often diverge from those of the United Kingdom. Garret Fitzgerald, the former Taoiseach, has argued that Northern Ireland's interests could be secured by their representation via participation in the Republic's involvement in the Community. Put simply, Northern Ireland could remain in the United Kingdom but be part of Ireland for EC purposes.[3] Although such a development is highly unlikely, the Dublin government has on occasion mediated in EC negotiations that had implications for Northern Ireland. In fact, the granting of a third seat to Northern Ireland owes something to pressure put on the British negotiators by the Republic's government to ensure that the nationalist population would have a representative in Strasburg. Moreover, there is co-operation between Dublin and London on agriculture and fisheries, for example. The Community's policies on cross-border co-operation, notably the INTERREG programme, have led to low-key co-operation between both parts of the island.

Conclusions

Since 1973, membership of the EC has involved the Irish state in an increasingly interdependent regional economy and in an evolving political system above the level of the state. This has afforded some opportunities to manage the impact of an increasingly globalised world economy. The EC, based as it is on a system of law and institutional procedures, offers small states an opportunity to wield influence in a world of unequal power. There has been a gradual 'Europeanisation' of Irish government and politics. This is set to continue with the deepening of integration. EMU will have considerable impact on macro-economic management in Ireland; it will affect budgetary politics and relations between government and the social partners. A common foreign and security policy will strengthen the regional character of Irish foreign policy and may in time lead to the Republic's involvement in a security pact. European integration has changed the context of both Anglo-Irish and North-South relations.[4] It has not, however, lessened the conflict in Northern Ireland about its future constitutional status.

Notes

1   Hainsworth, P. (1989), 'Political parties and the European Community' in Aughey, A., Hainsworth, P., and Trimble, M. J., *Northern Ireland in the European Community: an Economic and Political Analysis*, Policy Research Institute, Belfast, pp. 51–72.

2   The synthetic index is explained by R. T. Harrison, 'Northern Ireland and the Republic of Ireland in the Single Market' in Foley, A., and Mulreaney, M. (eds.), *The Single European Market and the Irish Economy*, IPA, Dublin, 1990.

3   *Irish Times*, 16 July 1991.

4   Laffan, B. (1992), *Co-operation and Integration in Europe*, Routledge, London.

Local government

Introduction

Even a cursory study of local government systems throughout Europe indicates that there are many variations between countries.[1] Each individual state, while conforming to some general norms of service delivery and local decision-making, tends to introduce some particular features of its own. This chapter describes two distinct systems of local government within Ireland which have evolved and been influenced by different circumstances.

In so far as the Republic is concerned, the system is fundamentally that established by the Imperial Parliament of the nineteenth century, in particular the Poor Relief Act of 1838 and the Local Government (Ireland) Act of 1898. Some variations have been introduced since 1922, but the influence of these earlier statutes and the dominant position of the county council still remains.

Local government in Northern Ireland, before 1973, was also a product of the 1898 Act, which created an administrative framework similar to the English council system. By 1921 the two-tier structure comprised two county boroughs, Belfast and Londonderry, and six county councils acting as a top tier, with a lower tier of urban and rural district councils. After 1922 the Unionist government consolidated its grip on local government by the Local Government (NI) Act (1922), which replaced proportional representation by majority voting, re-drew ward boundaries and altered the franchise by incorporating property ownership as a qualification for the vote.[2] Although local government in Northern Ireland experienced pressure to reform from 1940 onwards, due mainly to the large number of small inefficient local authorities, it was not until the late 1960s that proposals for change emerged.

The two systems of local government can be usefully examined under the headings:

1   Form – structures or types of authorities;
2   Functions – the actual services and the manner in which they are provided;
3   Finance – how the authorities are financed, whether by rate, or government grant, which would imply consideration of the relationship with central government and of course charges for services.

Form

Northern Ireland

The present structure of local government in Northern Ireland is a product of the Local Government Act (Northern Ireland) 1972. Twenty-six local councils were created, based on district town centres, for the provision of minor services. In the pre-1972 era a two-tier county/district structure existed with seventy-three elected authorities, which proved neither administratively nor financially viable. Political criticisms over the local government franchise and housing allocation practices also conspired to provide a complete overhaul of the administration and delivery of public services in the late 1960s and early 1970s. The removal of housing as a local government function, the abolition of Stormont in 1972 and Direct Rule all had an impact on the present structure of councils. Major services, such as education, housing, health, roads and water, are administered directly through government departments or centralised boards ultimately under the control of the British government working administratively through the Northern Ireland Office. Minor functions, discussed below, are under the control of district councils.

Structural arrangements for local government are inseparable from the political format and party system which provide the context for local service delivery. Elections for the new councils first took place in May 1973 and are held every four years under the single transferable vote (STV) system of proportional representation (PR). The resultant pattern of political control since then reflects the PR system, in which few councils are controlled outright by one party and a greater spread of minority representation exists. Table 4.1 illustrates the voting patterns over the five council elections held since 1973.

On the Unionist side, there has been a steady growth and then decline in support for the DUP at a local council level, whilst the UUP has consolidated its grip on local power. The emergence of Sinn Féin as a political party participating in the operation of local government has been a significant development in the nationalist camp. Sinn Féin's representation tends to be clustered in urban areas and their espousal of violence has caused much acrimony in council chambers. The 1989 elections were characterised by a contest for the non-traditional vote

Table 4.1 *Local government elections in Northern Ireland since 1973*
(*% votes*)

	UUP	DUP	OTH U	SDLP	SF	APNI	WP	OTH
1973	41.4	4.3	10.9	13.4		13.7		16.3
1977	29.6	12.7	8.5	20.6		14.4		14.2
1981	26.5	26.6	4.2	17.5		8.9	1.8	14.5
1985	29.5	24.3	3.1	17.8	11.8	7.1	1.6	4.8
1989	30.3	18.7	3.9	21.0	11.2	6.9	2.2	5.8

Note UUP = Ulster Unionist Party; DUP = Democratic Unionist Party;
OTH U = Other Unionists; SDLP = Social Democratic & Labour Party;
SF = Sinn Féin; APNI = Alliance Party for Northern Ireland; WP =
Workers' Party; OTH = Others.

in which the newly-formed Northern Ireland Conservatives successfully gained seven seats.[3]

There are 566 councillors in Northern Ireland for an electorate of 1,132,614. Excluding Belfast City Council, each council member, on average, represents 1,800 voters. This is a very generous ratio and contributes to the concept of localism, whereby councillors are accessible to their electors who can influence the decision-making process.[4] Local councillors in Northern Ireland attend to the queries or complaints they receive on issues over which they have no direct control, in particular housing. This can be frustrating for members who, in these circumstances, redirect queries to the relevant government departments or act as advocates for their electors. The paradox of the Northern Ireland system is that the administrative body with least functions – local government – is most accountable to the electorate and indeed represents the only democratic forum since the demise of the Northern Ireland Assembly in 1986. This has led to calls for increased powers by unionists although nationalists have opposed such a move. Frequent skirmishes between councils and central government over issues such as the Anglo-Irish Agreement and the presence of Sinn Féin members have not predisposed ministers to devolve greater powers.

Whilst there are no plans at present to create a new local government structure, two factors may contribute to changes in the council system. First, the Government appointed a Boundaries Commissioner in February 1991 to review the number, boundaries and names of local government districts and wards into which each district is divided. A review takes place every ten years. The Commissioner said at the outset that there were unlikely to be widespread changes, either in ward boundaries or in amalgamation of councils. His final recommendations in June 1992 included the retention of the existing 26 local government districts and an increase in wards from 566 to 582.[5] The second factor is the current talks on wider constitutional change. Any major developments on the broader political front are likely to influence the future role of local government.

The Republic of Ireland

In the Republic of Ireland the 1898 Act had a lasting influence on the structure of local government. Even when Independence was achieved in 1922, no fundamental changes were immediately imposed. This left in existence twenty-seven county councils and four county borough corporations (Cork, Dublin, Limerick and Waterford). Galway subsequently became a county borough under the Local Government Reorganisation Act of 1985. There still remain six borough councils within the county structure, Clonmel (Tipperary South), Drogheda (Louth), Dún Laoghaire (Dublin), Kilkenny, Wexford and Sligo. There are also forty-nine urban district councils scattered throughout the country in each county with the exception of Laois, Leitrim, Limerick and Roscommon. A number of *ad hoc* authorities exist, the most notable dealing with vocational education, the only real educational function provided by local government in the Republic. The Vocational Education Committees exist in each county, city and seven of the larger towns. There are eight regional health boards established under the Health Act 1970, slightly over half of whose members are nominated by local authorities. The health service is no longer legally part of the local government system even though it operated on a similar basis in relation to public accountability staff procedures and audit arrangements. The dominant influence on the structure of local government in the Republic is that of the county council, which still continues as the basic unit. An advisory group appointed in 1990 to report on local government reorganisation was requested not to interfere with the county unit, in so far as this was possible.

The management system in place in the Republic is clearly its best known feature. It has been called 'perhaps Ireland's major invention in the field of government'.[6] Certainly it has had a fundamental effect on the development of government in the Republic itself. As Lyons put it in a chapter entitled 'Building the New State': 'if that government gained in maturity and competence over the years the "managerial revolution" may take

a large part of the credit'.[7] Under the system, first introduced
in 1929, the city or county manager shares the power of the
local authority with the council. Each has distinct areas of
competence. The manager controls the local authority staff,
preparation of the budget and control of expenditure. The
councillors have power over general policy, which is reserved
for collective judgement. Over the years the managers and
politicians in the Republic have established efficient *modus
operandi* which successfully balance the needs of local democracy
and administrative efficiency.[8]

Functions

Northern Ireland

The key functions for which local councils have direct responsibility are technical, leisure, community services, building
control and environmental health. Technical services are
primarily concerned with street cleaning, refuse collection and
disposal but are also involved in maintaining council property
and minor works. This is normally a relatively large, labour
intensive service activity. Leisure services are provided as a
statutory function by councils. Facilities are as diverse as
the Dundonald International Ice Bowl and an aquarium in
Portaferry. A high level of provision in each district council
area has been assisted by large amounts of capital grant-aid
from central government and, in some cases, European funding.
Community services tend to concentrate their efforts on small-
scale provision in which assistance is given to local community
groups and voluntary organisations. The councils' community
workers act as facilitators for small groups in their dealings
with statutory bodies and encourage self-help. Councils are also
involved in the provision of community centres.

Building control and environmental health are not provided
on a single council basis (with the exception of Belfast) but on
a group arrangement. A number of councils collectively share
the expertise that could not be supported individually. Building

control covers the enforcement of building regulations through the examination of plans and the inspection of work on site at various stages of construction. Environmental health officers have an extensive brief to protect the public in areas such as food hygiene, air and water pollution, solid waste management, health and safety, and pest control and noise.

Apart from the functions outlined, local councils have become involved, since 1989, in the new function of community relations. Central government has supported councils financially, in the first instance for a three-year period, to employ community relations staff and offer support to cross-community activities. Councils have, therefore, been involved in developing schemes which:

- develop cross-community contact and co-operation;
- promote greater mutual understanding;
- increase respect for the different cultural traditions.

Some councils have also made extensive use of limited financial flexibility (under sections 107 and 115 of the 1972 Act) to assist local efforts at job creation and economic development. Against all odds, a number of local councils have also been very successful in the area of tourist development and associated economic spin-offs.

Aside from the role of directly providing the local services described, councils have three other functions – ceremonial, representative and consultative. Councils perform a variety of ceremonial duties, hosting civic receptions, conferring the freedom of the City or Borough on distinguished people, town-twinning and so on. Councillors sit as representatives on various statutory bodies to express views on the provision and operation of public services in their area. Examples of these include the five education and library boards, which have 40 per cent of their members nominated by district councils, and the four health and social services boards with 30 per cent council membership. Much controversy has arisen since April 1991 when, under new reforms in the health service, council representation was abolished. Local councils are consulted on the operation of regional services largely under the control of the central government Department of the Environment. Councils are approached for their views on proposals for capital schemes in water sewerage, the preparation of development plans, housing provision, redevelopment schemes and the acquisition of land.

A number of important changes are taking place which will affect the way in which local councils perform their duties. A draft legislative Order (Local Government (Miscellaneous Provisions) Northern Ireland Order 1992) has been circulated for consultation, the purpose of which is to bring local government in Northern Ireland into line with the rest of the United Kingdom. The new legislation will affect:

- the conduct of council business;
- the administration of environmental health and building control services;
- competition in the provision of district council services.

A new code of local government conduct for council members will be drawn up in consultation with district councils and a set of model standing orders established to regulate council business. Some of the standing orders will have statutory authority. Provision is also made in the new legislation for changes to the present group system which administers environmental health and building control. The proposals involve individual councils assuming responsibility for the appointment and employment of professionals in those functional areas with new mandatory joint committees based on areas conterminous with Health and Social Services Boards.

The most significant development is the introduction in late 1993 of competition into the provision of council services – compulsory competitive tendering (CCT). The new legislation will require the district councils to undertake the following activities only if they can do so competitively: collection of refuse; cleaning of buildings; other cleaning; catering; maintenance of ground; repair and maintenance of vehicles;

managing sport and leisure facilities, and construction and maintenance work. Local councils will have to compete successfully against private contractors for the provision of services, amounting to £100 million, before being allowed to undertake the function. This is a radical departure from existing practice and reflects similar obligations placed upon local authorities in Britain. The surprise in Northern Ireland is that the councils' role could be completely undermined with the contracting out of key services.

Republic of Ireland

The functions of local authorities in the Republic are classified into eight programme groups as follows:

1   Housing and building
2   Road transport and safety
3   Water supply and sewerage
4   Development incentives and controls
5   Environmental protection
6   Recreation and amenity
7   Agriculture, education, health and welfare
8   Miscellaneous services (financial management, elections, consumer protection, etc.).

The assignment of functions to local authorities does not accord with any general principle and is largely a matter of expediency or convenience.[9] In comparison with other countries in Europe, Ireland has very few local government functions.

As already mentioned there has been little 'root and branch' reform of local government in the Republic of Ireland since Independence. Some efforts have been made from time to time by successive governments during the last twenty years. Most recently, the Fianna Fáil/Progressive Democrats' programme for government (July 1989) promised the setting up of a select committee to examine and report on the whole question of local authority funding, structures and functions within a year.

A sub-committee of the cabinet was duly set up early in 1990 with an Advisory Expert Committee to advise it. Contrary to the popular assumption that public interest in or concern for local government was at a low level, the Advisory Group received a substantial number of submissions, almost 200, from a wide variety of interests. The Advisory Group's report was extensive, covering a wide range of issues, some fundamental, regarding the status and role of local government, including constitutional recognition, as well as topics such as adoption of the Council of Europe's Charter for Local Self Government. Disappointingly, finance – perhaps the crucial issue – was excluded from the terms of reference of the Advisory Group (apart from manner of distribution of state grants), as was the alteration of the county/county borough system itself. What might be regarded as a tentative first step towards reform appeared in the Local Government Act 1991, which was guillotined through Oireachtas (Parliament) before the local elections in June 1991. While silent on fundamental issues, the Act did include some significant provisions such as relaxation of *ultra vires*. Whether the report of the Advisory Group and the subsequent legislation represent a watershed is as yet uncertain.

It is impossible to consider the functions of local government in the Republic without reference to the high degree of control exerted by central government. As Marshall points out in reference to Ireland, 'central control is the most stringent of all'.[10] The origins of this go back to the founding of the Irish Free State in 1922. No recognition was given to the system in either the constitutions of 1922 or 1937. Within a year of assuming office and in the midst of a bitter Civil War, the government enacted the Local Government (Temporary Provisions) Act 1923, which extended to all local authorities the control previously applicable to Poor Law Guardians only. This copper-fastened central control legislatively and seems to have placed local authorities in a position of subordination. Financial problems, especially since the shortfall in domestic rate recoupment, created an increased dependency on central support and added further to central government control.

Finance

Northern Ireland

Unlike local authorities in Britain, councils in Northern Ireland have not been financed under the now discredited poll tax system. A two-part rating system is used to finance council expenditure:

- the district rate, which is set by each local authority to reflect net expenditure on its limited range of functions;
- the regional rate fixed by central government (the Department of Finance and Personnel) for services such as education, housing, personal social services, roads, water and sewage, not controlled by councils but which local people utilise.

The regional rate is struck at a uniform amount in the pound throughout Northern Ireland and district rates vary in each authority, reflecting different net expenditure incurred by individual councils.

The three traditional sources of income for councils are (a) rates, (b) charges for services, and (c) central government grants.

(a) Income from district rates represents around 60 per cent of local authority income. The district and regional rates are both collected (as a single bill) by the Department of the Environment (Northern Ireland) and the product of the district rate is paid over to each council.
(b) Charges for services rendered (e.g. trade refuse), facilities (e.g. leisure facilities) and work done (e.g. abattoir services) represent approximately 17 per cent of councils' income.
(c) There are three types of government grants: recoupment grants; percentage or specific grants; and a general grant. *Recoupment grants* are paid for services provided by councils on an agency basis, e.g. grass-cutting. *Percentage or specific*

grants are a proportion of approved expenditure on any one particular service, e.g. community services. Both these grants account for a small amount of councils' income – around 2 per cent. *General grants* are the principal grant towards the relief of rates which take account of (i) loss of rate income arising from industrial de-rating, and (ii) a resource element to help poorer councils afford a standard of service without the need to levy excessive rate poundage. The element varies from as little as 1 per cent for some authorities to 43 per cent for others. The general grant accounts for over 20 per cent of total council expenditure.

There is, therefore, an approximate 60:17:23 income split for district rates, charges and government grants respectively. Despite councillors having no control over the regional rate element they feel accountable for the total rates levied (regional and district rate), the major part of which is central government expenditure. The 1990/91 calculation for a domestic ratepayer illustrates the principle.

1990/91	£
Domestic regional rate	136.27
Average district rule	67.65
Total rate poundage	203.92

The average district rate represents one-third of the total rate poundage and the regional rate the remainder. Northern Irish councillors have argued that attempts by them to provide efficient services and a lower district rate are nullified by an increasing regional rate. Regional and district rates for the past seven years are illustrated graphically in Figure 4.1, which depicts the much larger increases in regional rate levels.

In line with changes to the poll tax, the Secretary of State for Northern Ireland announced in March 1991 that domestic ratepayers would have their gross rates bills for 1991–92 reduced

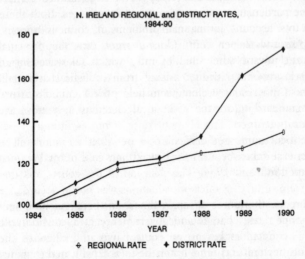

Figure 4.1 Northern Ireland regional and district rates.

by about 35 per cent, a proportion similar to that by which the community charge in Great Britain was reduced. The changes have been implemented by a reduction in the domestic regional rate and do not, therefore, influence the way in which councils budget for local services and strike a district rate.

The Republic of Ireland

The story of local government finance in the Republic is dramatic. The rating system had been under siege for many years and much dissatisfaction expressed from time to time. The farming community engaged in 'no rate' campaigns on a few occasions. Before the 1977 election, the Fianna Fáil party promised that domestic rates would be removed and taken over by the exchequer. That promise was accepted readily by the electorate and Fianna Fáil, returned to office by a large majority, duly removed rates from domestic property under provisions of the Local Government (Financial Provisions) Act 1978. A 100 per cent recoupment was statutorily promised to local authorities but over subsequent years this was reduced considerably. In 1983, to alleviate the financial problems of local authorities, wide power was given to introduce charges, especially for such items as domestic water supplies and sewage. These have been extremely unpopular and strenuously resisted. The charges still remain in most areas despite promises by the Fianna Fáil party in a manifesto before the 1985 local elections to remove the charges if returned.

The local authorities' difficulties were added to as a result of a court case taken by a number of farmers in County Wexford between 1982 and 1984. The decision of the courts was that the system of levying rates on valuations was not in accordance with the constitution. As a result, the landowners now no longer have to pay rates and the local funds are at a considerable loss. The State makes an *ex gratia* payment in lieu of the rates on agricultural land but it does not fully make up for the shortfall.

The present situation in relation to local finance and rates is most unsatisfactory. The search for an alternative source of revenue still goes on but a long-term and acceptable solution continues to be elusive. A limited residential property tax was introduced in 1983 providing for a tax at a rate of 1 per cent on the value of property in excess of £65,000 (annually updated for inflation and at 1991 rates are now £91,000), provided the annual household income exceeded £20,000 (£27,000 at 1991 revision). The yield from this tax has been quite disappointing and in its earlier years averaged only about £2 million annually compared with an estimate of £10 million. In recent years, the yield has been in the region of £4 to £5 million. This tax, of course, has been denied to local authorities and is paid on a self-assessment basis directly to the central exchequer.

The topic of local finance has over the years been addressed by various bodies, working parties and study groups (inter-departmental and otherwise), to little avail. One of the more serious studies was that published by the National Economic and Social Council (NESC) in May 1985. Having examined a number of options, the report concluded that it would be possible to devise a new local property tax which would avoid the shortcomings of the previous domestic rating system. No action has been taken as yet on this suggestion. Whilst a revised property tax cannot be ruled out on practical grounds, it is unlikely to be acceptable on political grounds. As the NESC study pointed out, 'Ireland is the only country where dwellings are generally exempt from a property tax and Ireland and the United Kingdom are the only countries where agriculture is exempt.'[11] In view of the problems which the poll tax caused in Britain, it is not likely to be introduced in the Republic and a return to the 'old-style' rates is also most unlikely.

Unless the problem of local authority finance is tackled successfully, the independence and viability of local government must be seriously called into question and any benefits from other re-organisation proposals seriously diminished.

Conclusions

While both systems of local government are different in terms of form, functions and finance, similar problems have emerged. Local government throughout Ireland is in a state of flux, with ongoing debates about the role of councils and their method of finance. The thorny issue of the relationship between central and local government is less problematic in Northern Ireland, where the broader political issues predominate, but it is nonetheless pivotal to the future status of councils in Ireland generally. The method of financing local government is currently under review and the rates issue has not been satisfactorily resolved in the Republic. Northern Ireland has escaped the debacle of the poll tax and council tax in Britain but considerable dissatisfaction exists over the regional rate. Local councillors feel accountable for this large element of government expenditure outside their direct control. The equivalent area of concern in the Republic is charges levied for local authority services. Not only has this created a rift between central and local government, but it has been singularly unpopular with the electorate. Local government throughout Ireland will, therefore, remain firmly on the political agenda.

Notes

1   Batley, R. and G. Stoker (eds.) (1991), *Local Government in Europe: Trends and Developments*, Macmillan, London.

2   O'Dowd, L., B. Rolston and M. Tomlinson (1980), *Northern Ireland: Between Civil Rights and Civil War*, CSE Books, London.

3   Knox, C. (1990), 'The 1989 local government elections in Northern Ireland', *Irish Political Studies*, V, pp. 77–84.

4   Jones, G. and J. Stewart (1983), *The Case for Local Government*, Allen and Unwin, London.

5   Hayes, M. (1992), *Review of Local Government Boundaries*, HMSO, Belfast.

6   Chubb, B. (ed.) (1964), *A Source Book of Irish Government*, Institute of Public Administration, Dublin, p. 261.

7   Lyons, F. (1973), *Ireland since the Famine*, Fontana, Glasgow, p. 484.

8   Collins, N. (1987), *Local Government Managers at Work*, Institute of Public Administration, Dublin.

9   Roche, D. (1982), *Local Government in Ireland*, Institute of Public Administration, Dublin.

10 Report of the Committee on the Management of Local Government (1967), *Management of Local Government*, IV ('Local Government Abroad'), HMSO, London, p. 24.

11 National Economic and Social Council (1985), NESC, Dublin, p. 70.

5 *Denise McAlister*

Public expenditure

Public expenditure is important to the Irish economy. In 1986, for example, it comprised 66 per cent of GDP in Northern Ireland and 58 per cent of GDP in the Republic of Ireland. Such magnitudes of public spending and implied levels of government involvement in the economy merit further comment and explanation. Given this rationale, the purpose of this chapter is to examine reasons for the growth in public expenditure over time; to outline and describe how such expenditure is more commonly defined and composed; to review the public expenditure systems in operation in Northern Ireland and the Republic; to highlight current issues and priorities, and identify future prospects and challenges. First, the chapter asks the question, 'Why are we interested in public expenditure, and in particular, the growth in public expenditure over time?' To some extent the range of possible answers is itself a reflection of the complexity of the topic.

The concern may be ideological. Libertarians, for example, may dislike the growth in public expenditure since it tends to limit freedom of choice and often has to be financed by taxes which are viewed as coercive. Such a view implies a political preference for a minimalist role for the government so as to curb the growth of state power whilst increasing that of private citizens and institutions. Those who view society in organic terms adopt a different perspective, claiming that market mechanisms, not public sector provision, need justifying, irrespective of questions of relative public and private efficiency.

Most individuals adopt a stance which lies somewhere between these two extreme views. It reflects the viewpoint in which Musgrave (1959) formalised the modern role of government in terms of the following trilogy: the allocative role, the stabilisation role, and the redistributive role.[1]

Musgrave pursued the idea that one should think of the budget office as being composed of these three functions. During the late 1960s and in the 1970s, and while the growth of public spending was accelerating, there was growing scepticism about government's ability to use the budget as an instrument for promoting the above mentioned objectives.

The allocative role was challenged by the perception of a public good being much more limited than had been originally assumed. It also became more difficult to separate the allocative from the redistributive objective in relation to particular services. Furthermore, government's ability at stabilisation policy was also seriously questioned with the coexistence of the phenomena of unemployment and inflation. Moreover, the latter two objectives are less convincing or justifiable in a regional context such as Northern Ireland where greater emphasis is placed on the efficiency properties, in terms of optimal resource use, of decentralised government (Tiebout 1956; Buchanan 1965; Litvak and Oates 1970).

Concerns about public expenditure growth may also arise in connection with the pursuit of macroeconomic objectives or microeconomic considerations. At the macro level, deficit financing may fuel inflationary pressures and/or cause a deterioration in the balance of payments. Even tax financing, through its impact on incentives, may inhibit the growth of private sector output. At the micro level there are concerns about the efficiency of public expenditure and the establishment of effective mechanisms for the appraisal, monitoring and control of resource use.

Various alternative explanations of the growth in the ratio of public spending to national income have been put forward.

Some of these theories are based on empirical evidence whilst others are based on political or ideological theory. While it is not the intention here to present an exhaustive survey of the theories which have been put forward to explain the growth in public expenditure, a brief review is warranted since economic and political groups will arm themselves with different arguments in order to bring about changes in policy.

Theories tend to be either demand- or supply-side viewpoints. A demand-side perspective was that of Wagner, a nineteenth-century German economist, which was based on the observation of a number of Western European economies. It predicted the growth of public spending on social services and transfer payments, infrastructure, and other economic services. The reasons for this were multifarious but included the proposition that as per capita national income rises, so the protective and social control activities of government would have to increase. This was because the fragmentation of social and economic life as a result of economic development would lead to greater social friction.

The growth of public expenditures on education, health and welfare services have been explained in terms of what economists call their 'income elasticities of demand'. Thus, as real income increases, public expenditures on these services rises more than proportionately, with the consequence that the ratio of government expenditure to GNP rises. For example, though health spending generally rises as a proportion of GDP as GDP itself rises, Ireland's health spending at 8 per cent is relatively high in OECD terms for its level of income or development.

A different perspective was suggested by Peacock and Wiseman (1961), based on a political theory of public expenditure. This approach views taxation as setting a constraint on government expenditures.[2] Using observations about the United Kingdom economy, Peacock and Wiseman contended that the growth in public spending over time had been uneven and had been pushed up in the twentieth century by social upheavals, in particular two world wars. They hypothesised that such 'upward displacement' takes place during social upheavals because there is an increase in the tax burden which society finds tolerable. Tolerable burdens of taxation increase due to two effects, the 'imposition effect' and the 'inspection effect'. The former refers to the possibility for government to impose new methods of taxation which in other circumstances would be unacceptable, and the latter to the tendency for government to identify additional social problems during the upheaval. As a result, there is the expectation that the government will continue to provide these additional public services. Such a theory may help to explain the rapid increase in public expenditure in Northern Ireland during the early 1970s, when the political disturbances highlighted the need for more public expenditure on social programmes as well as law and order.

Increasingly economists have sought explanations in conjunction with political scientists, sociologists, and others to explore hypotheses rooted in the behaviour of voters, politicians and public officials in democracies. The 'public choice' models (Buchanan and Tullock 1962) provide an alternative demand-side view.[3] Here the growth in expenditure is explained in terms of the effective lobbying by coalitions of voters who gain from expenditure on specific programmes, the tax costs of which are spread more widely. The net effect will be pressure to increase expenditure since the benefits to a particular group will exceed the tax costs. Expenditure is expected to grow until the median voter objects. Lindbeck (1985) has stressed the importance of special interest groups like farmers or home owners in the growth of horizontal redistribution, i.e. not to low income groups but to others who are able to organise themselves to retain or gain transfers and subsidies.[4] Musgrave (1985), however, highlighted the importance of anti-tax lobbies and concluded that the outcome of pro- or anti-spending lobbies cannot be determined a priori.[5]

A supply-side model much in vogue is that of Niskanen (1971), which emphasizes the role of senior officials in expanding government spending.[6] Here, like the voter and politician, the bureaucrat is viewed as having self-interests, which lead him to seek to maximise his own utility. Niskanen suggests that the elements in the bureaucrat's utility function include, *inter alia*, his salary, the size of staff working for him and their salaries, his public reputation, and his power or status. Since many of these items are directly related to the size of the budget, it follows that bureaucrats will also be budget-maximisers and, therefore, not neutral actors in the budget decision-making process.

The Niskanen model suggests that a public sector bureaucracy has a tendency to expand the level of output beyond that which is socially desirable. Such an analysis gives added impetus to libertarian demands to constrain the growth of the government by policies such as privatisation, cash limits and contracting out.

On a somewhat lighter note, support for the over-expansion hypothesis and the behaviour of bureaucrats comes from the BBC television programme *Yes Minister*. Jim Hacker, Minister for Administrative Affairs, is told by his political adviser: 'They (the civil servants) don't want cuts. ... Asking Sir Humphrey (Permanent Secretary) to slim down the Civil Service is like asking an alcoholic to blow up a distillery.' And on another occasion, Sir Humphrey himself confides: 'There has to be some way to measure success in the service ... the Civil Service does not make profits or losses. *Ergo*, we measure success by the size of our staff and our budget. By definition a big department is more successful than a small one. It seems extraordinary that Woolley could have passed through the Civil Service College without having understood that this simple proposition is the basis of our whole system.'[7]

None of the theories outlined above provides a wholly satisfactory explanation for the growth in public expenditure over time. This is not surprising since, to some extent, the differences in approach may reflect the search for answers to slightly different questions.

Decisions on the total of public expenditure each year will be strongly influenced by the implications for taxation and borrowing. In other words, at a national level, public expenditure decisions will tend to be revenue-based. The composition and level of spending are determined by the prevailing political and economic wisdom about the desirability of public expenditure, an estimation of the most appropriate level for such spending and the view adopted as to which services are best supplied by the government via the public sector.

Public expenditure can be defined, measured and analysed in various ways, the most appropriate measure depending upon the question to be answered. For example, if the principal focus of political and popular debate is on relative public spending priorities, then public spending by programme, e.g. health, law and order, social security and welfare, is the relevant measure. Alternatively, if the interest is in the appropriate division between private and public uses of resources, then the focus should be on public spending by economic category since the latter distinguishes between government spending on goods and services, and transfer payments. If, however, the concern is the amount of public expenditure to be financed, then it is the total amount of expenditure that is relevant, irrespective of its economic composition, or who is responsible for spending it.

Likewise, a number of different methods can be used to define the public expenditure aggregate itself. In the context of the United Kingdom, at least three definitions may be distinguished: general government expenditure as defined in the National Income Accounts, public expenditure as a planning total, and supply expenditure.

The absolute amount of public spending is a meaningless concept until it is seen alongside other magnitudes, such as the size of the economy as a whole. The relative size of the public sector is usually measured by comparing public expenditure with some national income aggregate. The importance of a sector is measured by the contribution it makes to the final output of the domestic economy over a defined period of time usually measured in terms of Gross Domestic Product (GDP). This is the most popular measure of the relative importance of the public sector, despite definitional problems and other technical difficulties associated with its use. Definitional changes cause problems for those who wish to analyse trends over time or to make international comparisons. These comparisons are made more difficult by the need to distinguish between changes in expenditure which have arisen due to changes in the price of public sector output, and changes in the volume of public sector output.

Price changes in turn can be divided into those due to general inflation and those due to relative price changes. In the economy as a whole, general inflation is measured by the growth in the GDP price deflator. Government spending which is reduced by the GDP deflator is referred to as spending in 'real' terms and is a measure of the opportunity cost of public spending in terms of other uses of GDP foregone after allowing for general price increases.

The growth in public spending in real terms can be viewed as being comprised of two elements: a change in the volume of inputs (like numbers employed) and changes in their relative prices. Since inflation does not affect all prices to the same extent, the prices of goods and services bought by government may rise faster or slower than the prices of goods and services as a whole. The effect of these relative price changes can be removed by applying their own price deflators, which produces expenditure at 'constant' prices or in 'volume' terms. Thus, the increase in government spending as a share of GDP at current prices may be decomposed into the effect of growth on input volume, the effect of price increases on initial volumes, and the combined effects of increased volumes at increased prices.

In practice, there has been a tendency for the prices of the inputs into government current expenditure to rise faster than GDP prices generally. One possible reason for this is that opportunities for introducing new, productivity-increasing techniques into public sector activities may be limited due to their labour-intensive nature. Despite, for example, advances in educational technology, the process of teaching a class requires the same quantity of labour input as it did twenty-five years ago. The implication of the relative price effect (RPE) is that the share of government expenditure on goods and services in GDP tends to rise faster in current prices, which is what matters for financing, than in volume terms.

Money to finance public spending can come from a variety of different sources including the sale of goods and services by public bodies, money raised by local government through local taxes and charges for services, privatisation proceeds or government borrowing. The bulk of the money is, however, raised through central government taxation.

A comparison of the tax systems reveals sharp differences between the Republic of Ireland and Northern Ireland. (See Chapter 4 for a comparison of government finances.) In the former the tax base is very narrow and, compared to the United Kingdom, yields from corporation and property taxes are low. The Republic's government is committed to broadening the tax base, thereby allowing correspondingly lower tax rates and shifting the tax burden away from personal income. Recent budget adjustments reduced the standard rate of income tax to 27 per cent and the single higher rate to 48 per cent, as well as increasing the middle VAT rate to 21 per cent. These changes bring the Republic closer to UK rates of 25 per cent, 40 per cent, and 17.5 per cent respectively. These figures do not in themselves, however, highlight a major problem with the Republic's tax system, which is that modest incomes are being taxed at the higher rate. In Northern Ireland, for example, a single person is allowed to earn a sum of £3,445 tax free and can also earn up to £27,145 without exceeding the standard rate of 25 per cent, with the balance of income taxable at only 40 per cent. In the Republic, the comparable figures are £2,175 tax free, income up to £9,850 payable at 27 per cent and the balance taxable at 48 per cent.[8]

The mechanics of raising central government taxes is centred on the Finance Bill, which is considered by the national legislatures each year. Without the passing of this Bill, government cannot raise the necessary cash to finance public expenditure.

Public expenditure in Northern Ireland

In Northern Ireland, the public expenditure arrangements are expenditure- rather than revenue-based. Unlike the British or the Republic's governments, the need to raise revenue via taxes and the other sources referred to earlier to pay for public expenditure is missing. The origins of the current arrangements were established in 1921. The recent arrangements reflect failure to produce a successor to Northern Ireland's own elected legislative assembly.

Under the Government of Ireland Act 1920, which established legislative devolution, Northern Ireland was expected to meet all its domestic expenditure and make a contribution to central costs such as defence. Despite the provisions of this Act, which included the power of granting relief from income tax and super-tax in Northern Ireland, it soon become apparent that, with the same tax and benefit rates, such an obligation could only be fulfilled if Northern Ireland operated at lower levels of public service provision than those prevailing in the rest of the United Kingdom:

The underlying premises were that Northern Ireland might not choose to provide its citizens in every respect with the same standards of living and services as in Great Britain, that it might indeed choose to stimulate its economy by holding back taxation levels, but that nevertheless on the basis of prudent administration it would be able to 'live off its own resources'.[9]

In practice, the financing of social security transfers proved particularly problematic since the responsibility for these benefits, retained by Westminster in the 1914 Home Rule legislation, had been devolved in 1920. Northern Ireland was thus at a disadvantage compared with other UK regions.

During the 1930s the principle of 'parity' was conceded. The acceptance of this principle meant that payment of taxation at the same rates as those in the rest of the United Kingdom implied an entitlement to expenditure on a common scale. This was to be related to needs and to the differing relative costs of providing such services. In the 1950s it was further conceded that extra provision should be made in Northern Ireland for past accumulated deficiencies in the social programmes and as compensation for Northern Ireland's geographical disadvantage within the UK.

In the 1960s, public expenditure per capita was still below the figure for England. Whilst progress was made in the late 1960s and early 1970s, public expenditure per head in Northern Ireland lagged behind that for Scotland and Wales. In 1972, when devolution was replaced by Direct Rule, spending increased sharply. Westminster was now responsible for the deficiencies and was hopeful that if these were made good, social tensions might reduce. Public spending, in real terms, in Northern Ireland approximately doubled in the twenty-year period from 1968 to 1988. The most dramatic period of growth occurred between 1972 and 1976, when public expenditure grew by 33 per cent. As mentioned previously, this period coincided with the introduction of Direct Rule and reform of the public finances contained in the Northern Ireland Constitution Act 1973.

Increasingly, the relative spending position of Northern Ireland, still the poorest of the UK regions, is being subjected to greater scrutiny and question. New evidence points to public spending in Northern Ireland being about 18 per cent higher than the average for the United Kingdom as a whole. Comparison is difficult, however, due to lack of comparable statistics, and the problems encountered in assessing need. Assessments by the Northern Ireland Economic Council (NIEC) conclude that the higher public expenditure in Northern Ireland can be satisfactorily explained by greater needs. Recent need factors identified which contribute to the higher per capita spending include: differences in administrative arrangements; public sector housing; demographic structure; the size of the agricultural sector; and the demands on law and order provision.[10]

Consequently, the revenue base in Northern Ireland, in common with other UK regions, is insufficient to sustain current levels of spending. Quigley comments that if Northern Ireland were self-financing in terms of the programme of public expenditure, then local spending would have to be cut by one third.[11] Such concentration on government transfers places Northern Ireland in a vulnerable position with regard to possible reductions in UK benefits. However, as Wilson argues, 'It is also true that this insecurity may simply be ignored for a long time and there may be an inclination to assume that, in so far as their own efforts are inadequate to meet their "needs", the deficiency will always be made good by Whitehall.'[12]

The growing dependence of Northern Ireland on subventions from Westminster may be contrasted with the Republic of Ireland, which became increasingly dependent on debt. This arose partly in response to higher levels of social benefits which were not tax financed. The public debt had risen in the mid-1980s to roughly £21,000 per employed person, with about 40 per cent owed abroad. As Bradley shows, the debt burden in Northern Ireland would be even greater had it not been for the Westminster subventions and ignoring the even higher social expenditure than the Republic[13].

Northern Ireland's allocation of resources is determined each year as part of the annual Public Expenditure Survey for the United Kingdom. The system of annual surveys for planning public spending has developed over the past twenty-five years and had its origins in the 1961 Plowden Committee Report. In the Survey, the government decides what total spending should be and how that total should be allocated between different services. The results of the Survey, including the total spent in Northern Ireland, are announced in summary form in the Chancellor's Autumn Statement. Allocations to individual Northern Ireland programmes are announced by the Secretary of State for Northern Ireland soon after the Autumn Statement.

Since the introduction of Direct Rule in 1972, the Secretary of State has been responsible for the governance of Northern

Ireland, supported by a number of ministerial colleagues. The resources available to the Secretary of State constitute an 'Expenditure Block' which is a flexible regional resource. The Northern Ireland Block grant has three main components:

(i)   expenditure on law, order, protective and miscellaneous services by the Northern Ireland Office (NIO);

(ii)   expenditure by Northern Ireland Departments, including the external financing of Northern Ireland Electricity, the Northern Ireland Housing Executive, the Northern Ireland Transport Holding Company, the Laganside Corporation and the public trust ports;

(iii) central government grants to District Councils.

Within the total resources available to him, the Secretary of State has considerable discretion to plan the level of expenditure in response to local needs and priorities, albeit within the framework of UK-wide policy. Within the Block, expenditure on social security is 'ring fenced' so that its level does not affect the resources available to other Northern Ireland programmes. In practice, however, the room to manoeuvre is limited. A large proportion of the Block goes on expenditure on wages and salaries which, in the case of labour-intensive programmes like education and health, are determined by the level of pay settlements in the United Kingdom.

The Northern Ireland Block should be distinguished from the Northern Ireland programme. The latter includes expenditure by the Department of Agriculture Northern Ireland (DANI) on agricultural and fisheries support. Neither the Northern Ireland Block nor the Northern Ireland programme includes expenditure incurred in Northern Ireland by other UK departments for which other ministers have responsibility, e.g. expenditure on the British Army, including the Royal Irish Regiment, and the Northern Ireland Court Service are the responsibility of the Ministry of Defence and the Lord Chancellor respectively. Furthermore, since all payments to and receipts from the European Community are taken into account when decisions are made about levels of public expenditure in the United Kingdom, the planned level of spending in Northern Ireland reflects expected receipts from the European Community's structural funds and other EC sources.

In the annual Survey process, co-ordinated by the Department of Finance and Personnel, changes to the total provision for the Block are largely determined through the principle of comparability with Britain. The Northern Ireland Block is adjusted either up or down in line with movements in comparable programmes in Britain. Northern Ireland's share of these spending changes is based on the 'Barnett Formula', a population based ratio attracting an allowance of 2.75 per cent of the total for comparable programmes in England. In the light of the publication of recent census figures this ratio has been increased to 2.87 per cent. Other changes to the Block provision can be made in response to the particular circumstances prevailing in Northern Ireland, as well as the UK public expenditure climate.

Each Survey looks ahead over a three-year period. Plans for the first year, which in the case of the 1992 Survey is 1993/4, need to be precisely drawn, whilst those for the next two years will necessarily be more tentative and will be reviewed again in the course of subsequent Public Expenditure Surveys. For a full account of the main stages in a typical Survey see Quigley (1987).

The more recent Public Expenditure plans for the Northern Ireland programme, that is, total expenditure within the Secretary of State's responsibility, were announced in the Chancellor's 1992 Autumn Statement and are as shown in Table 5.1. Allocations to individual programmes for the period 1992/3 to 1994/5 are shown in Table 5.2.

As in the United Kingdom, the largest item of expenditure is on social transfers, such as pensions and unemployment benefit, which accounted for about 31 per cent of the total in 1992/3. If expenditure on health, education and housing is added, the cost increased to some 69 per cent of total public expenditure. Law and order accounted for another 12 per cent. By comparison, industry, energy, trade and employment comprised 6 per cent of the total.

Table 5.1   *Total provision for the Northern Ireland programme,*
1992/93–1994/95

| | Plans (£m) | |
1993/94	1994/95	1995/96
7,460	7,690	7,940

Note Figures are rounded to the nearest £10 million.
Source Chancellor's Autumn Statement, Northern Ireland
Information Service, 8 November 1992.

Strategic public expenditure priorities, of which there are
currently three, are set out by the Secretary of State:

- to end terrorism and, in the meantime, to secure a
  continuing reduction in the levels of violence;
- to strengthen the Northern Ireland economy by fostering
  greater industrial competitiveness and higher levels of
  enterprise and initiative;
- to continue to attach great importance to the social
  programmes, including education, health and housing,
  improving community relations and equal opportunities.

It is difficult to relate differences in resource provision
directly to output priorities. Concern over the provision of
a service need not, at the margin, imply increased spending
if efficiency can be improved. The scope for efficiency gains
varies widely between programmes. Furthermore, programmes
may also differ in the extent to which they may be varied in
the short run. In programmes such as health, education and
social welfare, publicly stated policy commitments, demographic
influences, statutory requirements and the influence of pressure
groups in practice constrain a Secretary of State's or Minister
for Finance's ability to manoeuvre.

Expenditure on housing in Northern Ireland provides a neat
example of how priorities can change significantly over time. In

Table 5.2 *Planned public expenditure in Northern Ireland, 1992/93–1994/95*

Programme	1992/93	1993/94	1994/95
Northern Ireland Office:			
Law, Order, Protective and Miscellaneous Services	832	880	920
Northern Ireland Departments:			
Northern Ireland Agriculture, Fisheries and Forestry Services and Support	119	120	130
Industry, Trade and Employment	445	440	440
Energy	5	0	10
Transport	173	180	190
Housing	249	260	270
Environmental and Miscellaneous Services	199	230	240
Law, Order and Protective Services (Fire Service)	37	40	40
Education	1211	1270	1330
Health and Personal Social Services	1242	1290	1340
Social Security Administration	150	150	150
Other Public Services	90	90	100
TOTAL NI BLOCK (excluding Social Security Benefits)	4754	4970	5150
Social Security Benefits	2177	2350	2490
TOTAL NI BLOCK	6931	7320	7650
National Agriculture and Fishery Support	94	90	90
TOTAL NORTHERN IRELAND PROGRAMME	7025	7410	7740

Notes
(a) Figures are rounded to nearest £1m for 1992/93 and to the nearest £10m for 1993/94 and 1994/95 (thus £0 means less than £5m). Figures may not sum to totals due to roundings.
(b) The PE plans for 1992/93 onwards have been adjusted to reflect Government's intention that NIE should be privatised early 1992.
(c) The planning figures for 1992/93 form the basis for preparation by Northern Ireland Departments and Northern Ireland Office of Main Estimates for the coming year. These will be presented to Parliament in due course.
Source: Chancellor's Autumn Statement, Northern Ireland Information Service, 6 November 1991.

the 1970s and early 1980s housing enjoyed a high priority due
to the relatively poor housing conditions. Between 1980/1 and
1985/6, there was an increase of 22 per cent in real terms
in gross expenditure on housing. As the increased spending
began to impact upon housing unfitness, expenditure on
housing declined from 8 per cent of the public expenditure
total in 1983/4 to a planned 3.5 per cent of the total in
1992/3[14].

Given the dependence of the Northern Ireland economy
on the public sector, privatisation policies aimed at reducing
that dependence have been welcomed and encouraged by
government ministers but strongly criticised by local politicians
and trade unionists. Harland & Wolff and Short Brothers have
already been privatised, the former as a result of a management
buy-out, while the latter was sold to a Canadian company,
Bombardier Inc. Furthermore, Northern Ireland Electricity
(NIE) is to be transferred to the private sector, as part
of the UK policy to privatise the energy industries. The
privatisation programme is to be extended with the recent
ministerial announcement that Northern Ireland Airports Ltd.
(NIAL) is the next agency to be privatised. These follow earlier
initiatives to privatise services where pressures have been exerted
on Health and Education Boards to test the cost-effectiveness of
services by putting them out to competitive tender.

Public expenditure in the Republic of Ireland

Unlike Northern Ireland, where such decisions are expenditure-
rather than revenue-based, policy on public expenditure is part
of the overall economic and budgetary strategy of the Republic's
government. That strategy is to promote:

- a stable competitive environment;
- a low-inflation economy;
- commitment to maintenance of the value of the Irish pound
  in the EMS;

- a public debt which continues to decline as a percentage of GNP, lessening the burden of debt-service and the associated need for taxes;
- structural reforms to help growth and maximise its employment-intensity.

The performance of the Irish economy over the period 1986–92 has been impressive, especially when viewed against the poor performance of the first half of the decade, when the scale of unemployment and the imbalances in the public finances were a matter of serious concern. Compared to the period 1980–86, when the growth rate was barely above zero, GNP has grown at an average annual rate of 3.6 per cent. Inflation is below both the EC and OECD average. The national debt/GNP ratio and the Exchequer Borrowing Requirement (EBR) have fallen, the latter from 13.2 per cent of GNP in 1986 to an estimated 2.9 per cent in 1993.

The progress which was made coincided with the Programme for National Recovery (PNR) which the Government agreed in 1987 with the social partners. The Programme provided for reductions in the EBR and the national debt/GNP ratio, moderation of pay increases, lower inflation and interest rates, and linking the exchange rate to the European Monetary System. The extent to which the latter caused the strong economic performance in the 1988–90 period is debatable since it is not clear that, in the absence of the PNR, budgetary policy would have been any different. Nevertheless, the fact that, following the demise of the PNR in 1987, it was replaced with a similar consensus approach to economic management under the auspices of the Programme for Economic and Social Progress (PESP) suggests that the potential political and economic benefits of such programmes are viewed as significant.

Like most other Western European economies, the development of the Republic's economy has been accompanied by an increase in the amount of government involvement in the economy. The ratio of public expenditure to GNP has risen from 32 per cent in 1960, to 42 per cent in 1973 and 67 per

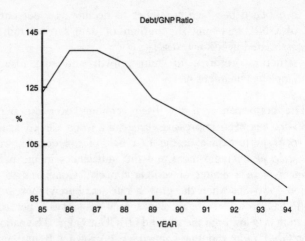

Figure 5.1 Debt/GNP ratio in the Republic of Ireland, 1985–94. (Source: ESRI Quarterly Economic Commentary, April 1990.)

cent in 1985. The main factors influencing the growth in public expenditure in the Republic have been national debt interest and social expenditure. In 1960 these two items comprised 50 per cent of the total, whilst in 1985 they had risen to 70 per cent. Since 1987 there has been a policy of public expenditure retrenchment and since then current public expenditure has fallen by over 11 per cent in real terms.

˜ A breakdown of how current expenditure is to be financed and allocated in 1993 is given in Table 5.3. Public expenditure comprises services which are met from the Central Fund and the ordinary day-to-day expenditures voted by the Dáil for public services. The 1993 estimate for the expenditure total is £10,480m. Central fund services comprise £2,902m of this, of which £2,490m is in respect of debt service payments. In 1991, the comparable figure for debt service payments was £2,409m and represented about 27 per cent of total current expenditure and almost 76 per cent of receipts from income tax. Figure 5.1 shows how the debt/GNP ratio has fallen from 138 per cent in 1986 to 107 per cent in 1991. Whilst the government remains

Table 5.3 How current expenditure will be allocated and financed in the Republic of Ireland 1993

Where current expenditure will go 1993 Post-budget	£M	Total gross expenditure (%)
Service of Public Debt		17.5
Interest	2260	
Sinking Funds, etc.	0230	
	2490	19.2
Economic Services		
Industry and Labour	0325	02.5
Agriculture	0526	04.1
Fisheries, Forestry	0037	00.3
Tourism	0026	00.2
sub-total	0914	07.1

How current expenditure will be financed 1993 Post-budget	£M	Total (%)
Current Deficit	0522	05.0
Tax Revenue		
Customs	0136	01.3
Excise Duties	1797	17.1
Capital Taxes	0079	00.8
Stamp Duties	0220	02.1
Income Tax	3563	34.9
Income Levy	0078	00.7
Corporation Tax	0867	08.3
Value Added Tax	2349	22.4
Agricultural Levies	0010	00.1
Motor Vehicle Duties	0235	02.2
Employment and Training Levy	0151	01.4
sub-total	9485	90.5

Table 5.3 Cont.

Where current expenditure will go 1993 Post-budget	£M	Total gross expenditure (%)	How current expenditure will be financed 1993 Post-budget	£M	Total (%)
Infrastructure	0078	00.6			
Social Services					
Health	1837	14.2			
Education	1705	13.2			
Social Welfare	3793	29.3	Non-Tax Revenue	0473	04.5
Housing	0004	00.0			
Subsidies	0170	01.3			
sub-total	7509	58.0			
Security	0940	073			
Other	1010	7.8			
Gross Expenditure	12941	100.0			
Supply Services Receipts	2461				
Total Net Expenditure	10480			10480	100.0

Source: Principal features of 1993 Budget presented to Dáil Eireann, 24 February 1993, Department of Finance.

committed to reaching its target of a ratio of 100 by 1993, and in the longer term to move the ratio closer to that of the other European countries, but such projections may turn out to be over-optimistic.

Nevertheless, national debt servicing has constrained the operations of fiscal policy and the heavy reliance on foreign debt has increased the exposure of the economy to international fluctuations in interest and exchange rates.

Within social expenditure, the largest item is income maintenance, which consists of social security and welfare payments and in 1993 will comprise 29.3 per cent of total gross expenditure. Combined expenditure on social services will consume 58 per cent of the total. By contrast public spending on security, and industry and labour will be 7.3 and 2.5 per cent respectively.

A study attempting to analyse the growth in expenditure over the period (1960–81) showed that the influence of the relative price effect was about one per cent per annum greater than the GDP deflator, though the effect was greater in education and health. By far the biggest component of the overall increase was the increase in the average real level of state expenditure per recipient. This was true for all the individual programmes, except for unemployment compensation in the period from 1975–81 when the growth in numbers employed predominated.[15]

In the early 1980s the Department of Finance introduced a new system involving the comprehensive presentation of public expenditure by programme to complement the traditional estimates and other budget publications. Since in the Republic of Ireland public expenditure management centres on spending departments, agencies, and their expenditure programmes, there is an incentive for programme and agency managers to exceed the resource constraint since such a system provides no mechanism for internal programme competition. In such conditions, if budgetary retrenchment becomes necessary, cutbacks may be imposed by central government, which given their lack of detailed information about individual programmes may not be in line with priorities. This problem has been partly

overcome by the introduction of the Expenditure Review Committee, initiated in 1987 by the Taoiseach, which required all Departments to carry out policy-based reviews of their expenditure programmes. As a result departments are forced to propose expenditure cuts or, more usually, defend their major spending programmes against the Finance proposals for reductions.

The NESC would welcome further public expenditure planning reform. In particular, they advocate the use of a total financial frame or block budget within which there is greater freedom to reallocate funds and adjust programme priorities. Such a system would also have to be accompanied by mechanisms which monitored performance. In addition, there is an argument for broadening the auditing remit of the Comptroller and Auditor General, as has been the case in Northern Ireland, to encompass assurances on efficiency and effectiveness as well as financial probity.[16]

Like Northern Ireland, the Republic has introduced policies directed towards improving financial management in the public sector. These have included:

- publication of the Comprehensive Public Expenditure Programmes;
- the fixing of administrative budgets on a three-year cycle with delegated managerial flexibility;
- guidelines on procedures for the appraisal of capital projects;
- the issue to departments of Guidelines for Financial Management;
- publication of a Government White Paper on Reform of the Public Service.

Future prospects and challenges

A recent economic history of Ireland provides a useful overview of what has been achieved, and more importantly, what are seen as key constraints to economic progress[17]. The Republic has achieved a considerable measure of economic development since independence. Such developments have helped to raise living standards, which are about three times higher on average than in the 1920s, accompanied by improvements in the levels of health, education and housing. When set in the European context, however, economic progress since independence is seen as mediocre. While the growth rate has been similar to the UK's, the latter was well below the growth achieved in many European countries. As a result the Republic's relative position in the European league, measured in terms of per capita GNP, has fallen.

Such mediocre performance must be viewed in the light of difficulties in the internal and external environment which lay in the way of Irish economic development. Nevertheless, the Republic's response to these obstacles has been far from effective. Kennedy *et al.* systematically query the oft-cited explanations which have been put forward at different times for Ireland's poor performance: high taxation, excessive government intervention, and wage increases that reduced competitiveness. Instead, they argue that the underlying reasons can be summarised as failure to grasp the implications of the small size of the country, lack of any long-term perspective and inadequate attention to human resources. Regardless of the arguments and notwithstanding the fact that economic progress has been made, the indigenous industrial base continues to be weak, and the problem of a surplus of labour has persistently remained despite substantial emigration. The ratio of debt/GNP is still a constraint. Turning to the question of future prospects for public expenditure, the outcome will depend partly on pressures from particular programmes and sectors, and partly on the government's overall stance towards public expenditure as part of its macroeconomic strategy.

Constraints arising from pressure on particular programmes are more likely to impact on public expenditure developments in Northern Ireland in the medium term. In particular, pressures for increased spending in the light of increased terrorist violence is likely to be significant. The extent to which other social programmes will be made to bear the increased cost of security programmes remains to be seen. Pressures to increase spending in areas such as health, education and economic development will themselves be substantial.

Historically, the performance of the Northern Irish economy has been linked closely to that of Britain. Despite the fact that Northern Ireland has benefited to some extent from growth in the UK national economy, high levels of unemployment have persisted. In fact for both Irish jurisdictions, economic performance, measured in terms of output and GDP, does not necessarily translate into jobs created.

For the Republic, the size of the National Debt continues to leave the economy and the public finances vulnerable to external interest and exchange rate changes. Moreover, debt servicing payments absorb resources which might otherwise be used to finance additional public services and/or reduce taxes. Additional pressure for public expenditure restraint is necessary if further progress is to be made with reform of the tax system and, in particular, the attainment of the Government's objective of 25 per cent standard rate of income tax and a single higher rate.

For both economies, the implementation of the Single European Market with movement towards greater monetary union, in conjunction with recent developments in Eastern Europe, will continue to be the strategic forces determining trends over the next five years. Reform of the CAP and the likely outcome of the GATT negotiations will pose challenges for the economy in general. Hence the success of recent strategies such as the PNR will need to be maintained if the Republic is to compete effectively in the changing international environment.

In practice, the challenge will be to strike a balance between the various priorities: providing additional jobs to cater for new entrants to the labour market as well as the unemployed; raising standards of living for those in employment; looking after the needs of those dependent on government support; and investing now for future prosperity. In striking such a balance, all areas of public policy and spending are likely to come under increased scrutiny.

Notes

1 Musgrave, R. (1959), *The Theory of Public Finance*, McGraw-Hill, New York. Under the allocative function, it is argued that certain goods referred to as public goods or merit goods cannot be provided through the market system because in some cases the market fails entirely, where in others it can function only in an inefficient way. Under the distribution function, a case for intervention can be made on the grounds of the unequal distribution of income and wealth. Finally, government action in the form of fiscal policy is required under the stabilisation function in order to ensure price stability and full employment.

2 Peacock, A. and J. Wiseman (1961), *The Growth of Public Expenditure in the United Kingdom*, Princeton University Press, Princeton; Allen and Unwin, London.

3 Buchanan, J. and G. Tullock (1962), *The Calculus of Consent*, University of Michigan Press, Ann Arbor.

4 Lindbeck, A. (1985), 'Redistribution policy and the nature of budget growth', *Journal of Public Economics*, XXVIII, 3.

5 Musgrave, R. (1985), 'Excess bias and the nature of budget growth', *Journal of Public Economics*, XXVIII, 3.

6 Niskanen, W. (1971), *Bureaucracy and Representative Government*, Aldine, Chicago.

7 Lynn, J. and A. Jay (eds.) (1984), *The Complete Yes Minister*, BBC Publications, London.

8 *Irish Times*, 30 January 1992.

9 Bloomfield, K. (1992), 'Constitution-making in Northern Ireland: a look around the monuments', *Business Outlook & Economic Review*, VI, pp. 35–50.

10 National Economic & Social Council (1990), *A Strategy for the Nineties: Economic Stability and Structural Change*, Dublin, Report No. 89.

11 Quigley, W. (1987), 'The public expenditure system in Northern Ireland', *Business Outlook & Economic Review*, II, pp. 27–32.

12 Wilson, T. (1990), Introduction in R. I. D. Harris, C. W. Jefferson and J. E. Spencer (eds.) (1990), *The Northern Ireland Economy:*

A Comparative Study in the Economic Development of a Peripheral Region, Longman, London, p. 12.

13 Bradley, J. (1990), 'The Irish economies: some comparisons and contrasts' in R. I. D. Harris, C. W. Jefferson and J. E. Spencer (eds.), *The Northern Ireland Economy: A Comparative Study in the Economic Development of a Peripheral Region*, Longman, London.

14 Connolly, M. and D. McAlister (1988), 'Public spending in Northern Ireland', *Public Domain*, Public Finance Foundation, pp. 140–49.

15 Maguire, M. (1984), 'Social expenditure in Ireland and other OECD countries: past trends and prospective developments', 'Public social expenditure – value for money?', papers presented at ESRI Conference, Dublin.

16 NESC (1990), *A Strategy for the Nineties*, p. 20.

17 Kennedy, K. A., T. Giblin & D. McHugh (1988), *The Economic Development of Ireland in the Twentieth Century*, Routledge, London.

References

Bradley, J. and J. D. FitzGerald (1990), *Medium-Term Prospects For Ireland: An Update, ESRI Quarterly Economic Commentary*, April.

Bristow, J. and D. McDonagh (eds.) (1986), *Public Expenditure – The Key Issues*, Institute of Public Administration, Dublin.

Buchanan, J. M. (1965), 'An economic theory of clubs', *Economica*, 32, 125, pp. 1–14.

Cm 1517 (1991), *Northern Ireland Expenditure Plans & Priorities; The Government's Expenditure Plans 1991–92 to 1993–94*, HMSO, London, February.

Kennedy, D. and A. Pender (eds.) (1990), *Prosperity and Policy: Ireland in the 1990s*, Institute of Public Administration, Dublin.

Levitt, M. S. and M. A. S. Joyce (1987), *The Growth and Efficiency of Public Spending*, National Institute of Economic & Social Research Occasional Paper XLI, Cambridge University Press, Cambridge.

Litvak, J. M., and W. E. Oates (1970), 'Group size and the output of public goods: theory and an application to state local finance in the United States', *Public Finance*, 25, pp. 42–58.

Northern Ireland Economic Council (1989), *Economic Assessment*, Report 75, Belfast, April.

Northern Ireland Economic Council (1991a), *Economic Assessment: April 1991*, Report 87, Belfast, April.

Northern Ireland Economic Council (1991b), *Economic Strategy in Northern Ireland*, Report 88, Belfast, July.

Northern Ireland Economic Council (1991c), *Autumn Economic Review*, Report 90, Belfast, October.

Programme for Economic and Social Progress (1991), The Stationery Office, Dublin, January.

Industrial development

Industrial development has been a key issue on the political agenda in both Northern Ireland and the Republic of Ireland since partition in 1921. From that time the expansion of the industrial base in both states has been recognised by all governments as a primary objective of policy. While it is commonly thought that what now constitutes the Republic was a largely agrarian economy until this century, there were in fact significant indications of industrialisation as far back as the eighteenth century.

O'Malley states that in the early nineteenth century Ireland had a fairly substantial industrial sector by the standards of that time and that in 1821 one-third of the Irish counties, including six out of twenty-three outside Ulster, had a greater number of people engaged in manufacturing, trade or handicraft than in agriculture. In 1841 one-fifth of the working population was reported to be occupied in textile manufacturing alone.[1]

Yet despite this early start, industrial activity declined at a rapid rate during the nineteenth century and with massive emigration the labour force of the twenty-six counties fell from 2.7 million in 1841 to just 1.3 million in 1911 – around the same level as today. Real efforts to promote a process of industrialisation did not occur until the Irish Free State was established in 1922. In contrast, in the six counties of Northern Ireland, industrialisation, in particular in the area around Belfast, has had a much longer and more continuous history, dating back to the development of first the cotton and then the linen industry towards the end of the 1770s. Moreover, unlike the rest of Ireland, the process of industrialisation continued during the nineteenth century with the development of the textiles industry being followed by a range of heavy engineering industries, including steam engines, boilermaking, shipbuilding and textile machinery.[2]

It is not the purpose of this chapter to discuss the various theories which have been put forward to explain the uneven development of industry in Ireland, although this is an interesting topic in its own right and one which has engendered a good degree of debate and continues to have some relevance to current problems.[3] The main focus here is the major issues which Ireland faces today in trying to develop industry to a scale which would enable it to compete more successfully in international markets and thereby create increased employment. In addition, the various policy responses which have been formulated by governments in both Northern Ireland and the Republic of Ireland over the recent past to achieve this objective are also discussed. While it would be wrong to try to understand current economic issues in Ireland without recognising, at least implicitly, the important political and historical developments which have brought us to the present situation, the focus in this chapter is much more on discussing current issues in Irish industrial development, both economic and political.

A major contention of the chapter, and one which underlies much of the discussion, is that despite the quite different historical experiences of Northern Ireland and the Republic of Ireland in relation to industrialisation both states now share similar industrial problems in terms of attempting to expand their respective industrial bases and being able to compete in international markets. In 1971 around 40 per cent of the work-force in Northern Ireland was employed in industry (in Belfast the proportion was even higher) but by 1990 this share had fallen to just 25 per cent.[4] Like other areas of the United Kingdom, such as Clydeside and the north-east of England, which had long been dependent on traditional heavy engineering, Northern Ireland has suffered a rapid rate of deindustrialisation since the mid-1970s. From around the beginning of the 1980s, however, manufacturing employment in Northern Ireland has largely stabilised, although it now has the smallest manufacturing sector in the United Kingdom outside the south-east of England. In the Republic of Ireland, on the other hand, there has been a steady increase in the numbers employed in manufacturing since the 1960s. While the rate of growth has varied over different periods, just as the rate of deindustrialisation was far from constant in Northern Ireland, the underlying trend has been one of general expansion. With the development of industry in the Republic, around one in five, the same ratio as in Northern Ireland, now work in manufacturing. In other words, disregarding the different composition of the respective manufacturing bases, the two states have now ended up with largely the same proportion of their work-forces engaged in manufacturing. Furthermore, although they have arrived at this situation from completely different directions, decline in Northern Ireland and expansion in the Republic of Ireland, they now share very similar economic and industrial problems.

While manufacturing output continues to grow, by 2.5 per cent per annum over the period 1985–90 in Northern Ireland and by over 8 per cent per annum in the Republic of Ireland, both economies have been unable to translate this growth into significant job creation. Over the same period manufacturing employment fell by around 2,000 in Northern Ireland and grew in the Republic of Ireland by just 4,000. As a result industrial policy, both north and south, has come under close scrutiny and its failings have been highlighted. During the 1980s, for example, it has been pointed out that manufacturing employment in Northern Ireland declined by 42,000 at a time when 'the two development agencies, the IDB and LEDU, spent over £1 billion on industrial development and claimed to have promoted over 74,000 jobs and renewed or maintained a further 100,000 jobs'.[5] Over the more recent period 1982–88 it has been estimated that less than 10,000 jobs assisted by the

IDB were still in place after six years, only 40 per cent of the jobs planned for and at a cost of over £600 million.[6] Moreover, these job creation figures did not allow for employment that would have been created irrespective of financial assistance (the deadweight effect) or the possibility that assisted employment was merely created at the expense of jobs lost elsewhere (the displacement effect). Looking at a longer period it has been estimated that 'only 65 firms employing 16,000 people remain to show (in 1986) for all the effort of industrial assistance from 1945 to 1973'.[7] This adds up to a fairly damning indictment of recent industrial policy in Northern Ireland.

In the Republic, the Telesis report commissioned by the National Economic and Social Council provided a wide-ranging review of industrial policy and concluded that 'only 30 per cent of the jobs approved in foreign-owned firms between 1970 and 1978 were actually on the ground in 1981 ... An even greater discrepancy exists for indigenous industry. Sustainable jobs as a percentage of job approvals is only 14 per cent ... The discrepancies are due mainly to company failures and employment losses in surviving companies'.[8] More recently the government concluded that 'it is clear that a poor correlation exists between State expenditure (direct and tax-related) on industry and net employment creation'.[9] This conclusion was confirmed by results from a study of the performance of grant-aided industry during the 1980s, which stated that 'Grants totalling (in 1990 prices) IR£530 million to foreign and IR£416 million to Irish-owned plants were paid during the decade to firms that existed at end-1980. Despite this, net job losses of 15,000 in overseas and 30,000 in Irish-owned plants occurred during the period in the firms to which the grants were paid.'[10]

Industrial policy

To understand why there has been such a poor industrial performance, and more specifically why industrial policy has failed, it is necessary to look in some detail at the respective policy responses in Northern Ireland and the Republic of Ireland. The key feature in this respect is that policy in both states has been highly interventionist in terms of the amount of resources which have been devoted towards industrial development. Indeed this has been to an extent almost unparalleled anywhere else in Western Europe, with the exception of some severely depressed areas such as southern Italy. The nature of this intervention in the economies of Northern Ireland and the Republic of Ireland while similar in framework has, however, shown some important differences.

Since the Second World War, a wide range of public assistance has been available for the development of industry in Northern Ireland. The most recent and significant form of such assistance was the establishment in 1982 of the Industrial Development Board for Northern Ireland (IDB), which took over and extended the role and policies of the Department of Commerce. In particular, the IDB was given the capability to fund industrial investment projects at anything up to 50 per cent of cost through selective financial assistance (SFA), mainly in the form of capital grants. In addition, or more accurately instead of SFA, any single investment project could be funded automatically under the Standard Capital Grants scheme at a rate of 20 per cent (the rate was reduced to 12.5 per cent between 1987 and 1988 and then abolished later that year). Moreover there are other incentives available to manufacturing firms in Northern Ireland such as corporation tax relief, full industrial derating, factory rental concessions and electricity subsidies. For small firms the Local Enterprise Development Unit (LEDU) was set up in 1972 and now offers a wide range of incentives for small business development similar to those offered by the IDB for larger companies. Together, this range and level of assistance has been described as 'the most generous and wide ranging package of incentives for industrial development of any region in the United Kingdom and possibly in Europe ... Compared with the average for all the assisted areas in Great

Britain, industrial assistance per capita in Northern Ireland was almost five times higher'.[11] Such a high level of assistance has led to the situation that 'no major industrial investment has taken place in Northern Ireland over at least the last ten years without a significant degree of public financial assistance'.[12]

In the Republic of Ireland the degree of industrial assistance, though somewhat different in nature, has also been substantial. The main body through which industrial policy is undertaken is the Industrial Development Authority for Ireland (IDA), which was established in 1949 with a very limited remit. Since that time its role has been expanded considerably and like the IDB and LEDU in Northern Ireland, the IDA has been given the capability to grant-aid industry, both large and small firms, to a substantial level. Before 1989 the IDA could fund all investment projects up to a limit of 45 per cent in most parts of the country and up to a rate of 60 per cent in certain designated areas. Since that time the upper rate of grant-aid has been reduced to 25 per cent for the expansion of firms already located in Ireland with a significant proportion of these grants made repayable (though not for foreign plants). The higher limits of grant-aid have been retained only for new greenfield projects. The major incentive for industrial development in the Republic has been the various forms of tax relief available. Until its abolition in 1978, after pressure from the EC, the Export Profits Tax Relief scheme allowed manufacturing firms which exported to pay no tax on profits earned. This was subsequently replaced by the Export Sales Relief (ESR) scheme which set a rate of corporation tax on profits for all manufacturing firms of 10 per cent up until the end of the year 2010. This compares with an average rate of corporation tax in the EC of around 39 per cent. The size of these incentives, especially those concerned with tax relief, highlights the huge benefits which accrue to multinational companies and largely explains the relative success of the IDA in attracting foreign investment to the Republic since the 1960s.

Current issues in Irish industrial development

What are the major issues which face industrial development in
Ireland today? It has already been suggested that the industrial
problems of the two states are remarkably similar but, at a more
specific level, the issues facing the respective governments in
attempting to further industrial development are also much
the same. The main distinction which needs to be made in
analysing industrial development in Ireland is that between
indigenously-owned industry and that part of the industrial
base which is foreign-owned, characterised in general by the
branch plants of multinational companies.

In the Republic the major focus of industrial policy since
1958, when the protectionist policies associated with de Valera
were largely abandoned and the so-called 'outward looking'
policies were introduced, has been the attraction of foreign
investment. From the early sixties and up to the present the
attraction into the Republic of foreign investment has been
viewed as an essential pre-requisite for the expansion and
modernisation of the industrial base. Foreign investment was
seen as the quick – though as was subsequently discovered
costly – route to attain late industrialisation for a small economy
on the periphery of Europe. In some respects this policy has
been successful, with foreign industry increasing its share of
total manufacturing employment from only 5 per cent in 1966
to 45 per cent in 1990. Almost 990 foreign firms now operate
in the Republic, employing 90,000 people and accounting
for 50 per cent of manufactured output and three-quarters
of industrial exports. Moreover, foreign-owned companies are
concentrated in high technology industries such as electronics
and pharmaceuticals, which together account for more than half
of total overseas industrial employment. The main origin of
the overseas investment has been the United States, although
companies from the United Kingdom, Germany, Canada, the
Netherlands, Sweden and Japan are also significant employers.
For much of the 1970s and the 1980s the success of the IDA
in attracting foreign investment led to the widely held view that

the Republic was the most attractive location for 'footloose investment' in Europe. The combination of high levels of grant-aid, a well-educated, English-speaking and relatively 'cheap and plentiful' labour force and, most importantly, very low, if not zero, rates of effective corporate taxation all made for an irresistible bait for many foreign companies which were looking to expand abroad.

The downside of the policy of attempting to attract foreign investment, however, was that the ultimate cost to government was extremely high. For example, the overall cost of the ESR and the variety of other tax relief schemes in operation was estimated for the year 1987/8 alone at IR£1,189 million, while for the five-year period 1983/84 to 1987/88 the cost of tax incentives was estimated at IR£3,766 million. In addition a significant proportion of the overall industry budget, which averaged over IR£273 million per annum between 1985 and 1989, would also be accounted for by expenditure on foreign investment.

Apart from the substantial cost to the taxpayer, other criticisms which have been made against the policy of attracting foreign investment are that the employment created is largely low-skilled and does not endure for long periods, as plants either close down or contract, and that few linkages are created with indigenous industry for the benefit of the rest of the economy. Furthermore, although a significant number of multinational companies have been attracted to the Republic, the characteristics of these branch plants are such as to make them little more than basic assembly units and, therefore, not central to the company's operations. Indeed, the very nature of the policy incentives used to attract such foreign investment, in particular the ESR scheme, encouraged this type of activity to locate in the Republic. The low, or in many cases zero, rate of corporate taxation meant that foreign companies would locate branch plants for assembly purposes, with the assistance of grant-aid, and with the very intention of importing most of their necessary inputs from other plants of the same company elsewhere in the world at artificially low prices. These plants then assemble and export the semi-finished product, with its much increased value-added and artificially high price, back to other overseas affiliates of the same company. This process of transfer pricing enables a multinational company, through its ability to undertake intra-firm trading and set its own prices, to exploit low tax countries and maximise profits. In other words, the wealth or profits which are created by the foreign-owned companies in Ireland are not reinvested back into the economy for its benefit but are sent abroad. So substantial is this factor that in 1990 profit repatriation totalled over £2.2 billion, around one-third of the output of the Republic's manufacturing sector or 10 per cent of the total GNP. If the figures for profit repatriation could be summed for the whole period since foreign companies first located in the Republic then the amount of direct wealth loss to the economy would be enormous.

An important ramification of the focus on foreign capital in industrial policy was that the potential and problems of Irish-owned firms were not given sufficient attention. It was not until the publication of the Telesis report in 1982 that the needs and difficulties of indigenously-owned companies were highlighted. In particular, Telesis stressed that because of the heavy emphasis on the attraction of foreign investment projects industrial policy had been insufficiently concerned with the development of large indigenously-owned Irish companies which could compete successfully in leading world markets. Telesis highlighted that not only had Irish-owned firms performed poorly in terms of output and employment growth, but that a major explanation for this was that such companies were heavily concentrated in traditional industries such as food processing, textiles or natural resource-based industries which had a low export propensity. Telesis concluded that 'no country has successfully achieved high incomes without a strong base of indigenously-owned resource or manufacturing companies in traded businesses'.[13]

Largely as a result of policy, but also because of longer-term structural trends, a dualistic industrial base had developed in the Republic. On the one hand there are a significant number of highly profitable branch plants of foreign origin which produce goods in many of the leading and high technology industrial sectors but whose wealth is largely exported. On the other hand Irish-owned companies have experienced a dramatic fall in their share of industrial output and employment largely due to their concentration in traditional and declining industries and their neglect by government. The effect of these trends was that by the mid-1980s the average profitability of foreign-owned firms was over twelve times higher than that of Irish-owned industry.[14]

Northern Ireland has also experienced the development of a dualistic industrial base, though not in quite as stark a fashion. The difference between the states is that while indigenously-owned firms in Northern Ireland are similar to those in the Republic in being largely concentrated in declining industries, Northern Ireland has been less successful in attracting such large amounts of foreign investment.[15] While there are, and have been, notable gains in terms of significant foreign investment projects, especially in the 1960s, the political situation has been a major impediment for the full promotion of foreign investment since the beginning of the 1970s. Moreover, the dramatic failures of a small number of large US-owned projects, such as De Lorean and Lear Fan, have highlighted the precarious nature of a policy which depends so heavily on foreign capital for industrial development. More recently the record of foreign investment projects in Northern Ireland has been particularly poor. US-owned companies, which were given large amounts of public assistance to set up by the IDB during the period 1982–88, managed to create only 8.5 per cent of the jobs they promised. This pushed the cost-per-job-created of these projects up to extraordinary levels. In the case of US-owned firms which were assisted by the IDB during the period 1982–88, the cost-per-job-created was estimated at over £205,000.[16]

Against the background of debate about the pros and cons of attracting inward investment and the continuing poor development of indigenously-owned companies in both Northern

Ireland and the Republic of Ireland, a number of new policy initiatives have been introduced. In the Republic, the IDA appears finally to have taken on board the findings and recommendations of the Telesis report and has belatedly recognised the need to develop a strong and indigenously-owned industrial base. In particular, the IDA appears now to realise that the task of developing industry in a late industrialising country is quite different from that of an economy which has been through a prolonged period of industrial growth. There is now a clear distinction in industrial policy in how foreign- and Irish-owned companies are treated. It is explicitly recognised that Irish-owned industry faces huge barriers to entry into international markets which only specific, focused and long-term public support can attempt to overcome. This 'structuralist' approach to industrial development, which has been strongly articulated by O'Malley, argues that latecomers to industrial development such as the Republic are unable to develop firms and industries to a size sufficient to overcome the high development costs of first entering and then subsequently competing successfully against international firms without substantial and specific public assistance.[17] Such barriers to entry include economies of scale, large capital requirements, product differentiation, advanced technology, specialised skills and the external economies inherent in large advanced industrial centres.

The importance of the structuralist analysis is that it recognises that traditional approaches to industrial policy, of the type both the Republic and Northern Ireland have followed for long periods, are misdirected. This is because they aim to tackle the conventionally understood constraints on industrial development such as lack of entrepreneurship, lack of capital, an insufficient physical infrastructure and a low quality labour force. While support for some, or even all, of these factors is necessary they are not sufficient to overcome the more deep-rooted structural problems of a late industrialising economy. Therefore, the appropriate policy response is one which is highly interventionist, and which will often go against the short-term dictates of the market, but also multi-dimensional in that a whole range of factors in the company and the industry are tackled at the same time. More specifically it is not sufficient merely to fund investment projects with straightforward capital grants or tax concessions. What is required is assistance across a range of activities such as marketing, product development, management skills and research development. An approach which itself requires a quite different and much wider range of skills on the part of the development agency. Importantly, the policy also has to be highly selective with regard to the firms and industries which receive assistance, thereby leading to a situation where public resources are concentrated in a few pre-selected industries and not, as before, spread thinly across the whole industrial base. Moreover, policy needs to be both long term and strategic in its outlook with assistance not being given to firms in order to tackle immediate short-term problems. Only firms which are seen as having a genuine long-term potential for success should be supported.

The IDA has apparently taken this thinking on board, although some would say rather belatedly and with little enthusiasm. It is now a clear objective of policy 'to increase by 100 within ten years the number of Irish manufacturing companies having an annual turnover greater than £5 million in real terms over the period'.[18] The overall level of industrial support has been cut considerably and those resources which are used are being targeted on a small number of pre-selected firms which are seen as having the real potential for significant and rapid development. The process is by no means complete, however, and industrial policy in the Republic seems to be forever under review.

At the beginning of 1992, a Review Group set up by the Government and composed mainly of industrialists published what has become known as the Culliton Report, named after the chairperson of the group. The key findings of this important report were that:

(i)   industrial policy had to be viewed in a much broader manner than previously and had to include the effect

on industrial development of policies on taxation, infrastructure and education and training;

(ii)   the economy needed much more market-led and
        production-oriented enterprise in contrast to the en-
        couragement of a 'hand-out mentality' or the promotion
        of unproductive activities;

(iii)   industrial performance had to be based on national sources
        of competitive advantage with Irish-owned companies
        requiring special attention; and

(iv)   the delivery of industrial policy had to be improved with
        greater cost-effectiveness and better monitoring.

A further important development since the late 1980s in the
Republic is that policy towards industry is now seen as a key
part of the wider consensual approach to economic policy, which
is most recently reflected in the Programme for Economic and
Social Progress. This approach aims to achieve agreement
amongst the so-called social partners, in particular the trade
unions and the employers, on the main parameters of economic
policy, but especially the annual rate of pay increases. It is
worth noting in this respect that the interventionist approach
to industry which the IDA now adopts at times appears to
conflict with the arms-length approach to overall economic
policy adopted by the Coalition governments of the late 1980s
and early 1990s. In the latter regard such a stance sees a
limited role for government in the economy and one which is
merely to create the right conditions from which growth will
apparently arise.

Continuing the theme of commonality between the north and
south on industrial development, debate about industrial policy
and indeed implementation in Northern Ireland has followed,
though much belatedly, the experience of the Republic. After
an attempt in 1987 under the so-called Pathfinder initiative
to change policy from its simple grant-giving focus, a more
serious review of policy began at the end of the 1980s and
culminated with the publication in 1990 of 'Competing in
the 1990s'.[19] While this document included much of the

rhetoric of the earlier, and now largely forgotten, Pathfinder document,[20] such as the need for more enterprise and an escape from a so-called 'dependency culture', the new strategy was centred around the two concepts of market failure and competitiveness. The first concept, in line with the way in which industrial policy had developed in Britain during the 1980s, saw government as having only a minimal role to play in the development of industry. The second concept of improved competitiveness was seen not just as the key objective of policy, although it has never been adequately defined, but also the criterion against which assistance for a project would be assessed and subsequently the means by which other benefits such as job creation would arise. The strategies which were subsequently produced by the IDB and LEDU to follow this new approach clearly showed the confusion and difficulty of trying to implement a policy based on free-market thinking into an economy which had experienced for such a long period substantial levels of industrial support. 'Competing in the 1990s' appeared to be suggesting a withdrawal by government from industrial policy, although the lack of seriousness in this respect was suggested by the fact that the annual budgets for the development agencies have subsequently continued to be increased in real terms.

In 1991 a report was produced by the government advisory body, the Northern Ireland Economic Council,[21] which seemed to offer a solution to the problems with which government and its agencies found themselves in terms of attempting to formulate a new industrial policy. Perhaps not surprisingly, the approach recommended by the NIEC, and which has apparently now been largely taken on board by government, is one which differs little from that being followed in the Republic by the IDA. The report recognised that the key problem of industrial policy in Northern Ireland, as had already been recognised in the Republic ten years earlier, lay with the difficulties involved in attempting to develop the indigenously-owned sector. Since most of the firms in this sector are small with a low export propensity, the new aim was to develop them to a scale sufficient for them to compete internationally. What was needed, as already recognised in the Republic, was direct and close intervention in a small number of companies which had a real long-term potential to grow, develop and create substantial employment.

Although the approach to policy is evolving at a slow pace in Northern Ireland and will take a number of years to take full effect (it has been suggested it took almost a decade for industrial policy in the Republic to change course and some would argue that this has yet to happen), industrial policy in the north and south is becoming increasingly similar. This is so even if the end result has been reached by different routes and for different reasons. In both states the underlying rationale for industrial policy is one that recognises the need to support indigenous industry and that the nature of that support, if it is to be really effective, needs to be specifically tackled and directed across a wide range of factors within carefully selected firms and industries.

As for policy towards foreign investment, there have been few changes in either the north or south of Ireland. In the Republic the tax limit was recently extended for a further ten years to 2010, reflecting the continuing priority that foreign investment has in industrial policy. However, more emphasis is now being given to encouraging greater links between foreign-owned branch plants and the rest of the economy so that increased multiplier effects can be achieved. Also there now appears to be greater concern for the need to get as much research and development and managerial activity located in the Republic as possible. The hope in this respect is that if a foreign company locates management with a fair degree of autonomy over the way in which the plant operates, and also locates key research and development functions which may determine the future operations of the company, then the long-term security of the plant in the Republic can be strengthened. In Northern Ireland, the recent review of policy had hardly anything of substance to say about the attraction of foreign investment.[22] As in the Republic, this is somewhat surprising given the chorus of criticism that has been directed against the experience of foreign capital locating in Northern Ireland. It appears, therefore, that foreign investment will continue to retain its high priority in industrial policy in Northern Ireland despite its substantial cost, its limited job creation record, and possibly the most important factor, the difficulty of attracting foreign investment given the current political situation.[23]

A major reason why the IDA and IDB continue to try and attract foreign capital to Ireland is that unlike policy towards indigenous industry, it is difficult to establish a midway stance. If a country or region gets involved in attracting foreign investment then there will be high costs because of the way in which incentives get pushed up by the beggar-my-neighbour policies adopted by almost all countries. On the other hand, if a country or region does not play the foreign investment game then it runs the risk of missing out on what can be a quick and relatively straightforward means of creating employment. Unlike attempts to develop indigenous industry, which can take decades before significant developments are seen, the attraction of foreign plants can have almost immediate impact. In this respect the benefits of such a policy are often not merely economic but also political.

Conclusions

As has been seen, industrial policy in Northern Ireland and the Republic of Ireland is a key economic and political issue and for at least two major reasons is likely to remain so. First, almost every economic and social indicator puts Northern Ireland and the Republic near the bottom of the European league table of relative prosperity. Unemployment remains staggeringly high (over 14 per cent in Northern Ireland and 20 per cent in the Republic); emigration continues, especially when fortunes improve in Britain and the US; growth in industrial output still has only a marginal impact on job creation; and perhaps most of all, the manufacturing sectors in both Northern Ireland and the Republic are still regrettably small in comparison with

Ireland's main competitors. There are now few who would argue, despite the growth in many countries of private services, that an economy can generate sufficient wealth in the absence of a strong export-oriented manufacturing sector.[24] The second reason why industrial policy will remain a key issue is that economies such as Northern Ireland and the Republic of Ireland increasingly have few policy levers which they can use to determine their economic destinies. In the case of Northern Ireland the economy is only a small component of the much larger UK economy, which means that developments are largely dependent on events occurring in Britain. Moreover, because Northern Ireland is only a regional economy it does not have any of the macroeconomic levers of policy available to it such as fiscal, monetary and exchange rate policy. In this way industrial policy is one of the few ways in which government in Northern Ireland can attempt to influence the regional economy. Indeed, the history and experience of industrial policy over the last forty years shows that Northern Ireland has been able to utilise a fair degree of autonomy over the way in which it has attempted to develop industry, both in the way in which policy is implemented and, more importantly, in the level of resources which it has been able to use.

In the Republic similar reasons can also be put forward for the continuing importance of industrial policy. While the Republic is a national rather than regional economy, it is very small in comparison with its main competitors, in particular other EC countries, and developments at the EC level, such as the creation of an integrated market and the proposed formation of a European Monetary Union, mean that even macroeconomic policy instruments are increasingly unavailable for effective use. Again, therefore, industrial policy is one of the few remaining areas of policy where government retains a degree of autonomy and can attempt to make an impact on the economy. If only for these two reasons, continuing economic deprivation and a lack of policy instruments available to determine economic development, it seems clear that industrial policy will remain high on the political agenda in Ireland for some time.

A major theme which has underlined this chapter is that Northern Ireland and the Republic of Ireland share many of the same problems in trying to develop their respective industrial bases. Moreover, the policies that have been developed to tackle these problems have slowly evolved in similar ways to the extent that it could be argued that the activities of the IDA and the IDB, are at least in framework, largely synonymous. It can also be argued that not only are the industrial problems faced by companies in Northern Ireland and the Republic of Ireland similar, but they have much more in common with each other than either does with areas in Britain.

In this context it would make economic sense if industrial policy could be operationalised, or at least co-ordinated, on an all-Ireland basis. A number of other factors also point to such a development. First, the creation of the Single Market means that the economic, though not political, divide between Northern Ireland and the Republic of Ireland will become increasingly less significant, making the island of Ireland much more like a single economic unit. Second, there is under current conditions a degree of duplication of effort, or rather wasteful competition, in terms of policy towards the attraction of foreign investment. Indeed, in some cases it can be argued that competition between the IDA and the IDB can actually bid up the cost of attracting an overseas project to Ireland. The third and possibly most compelling argument for recommending that industrial policy should be undertaken on an all-Ireland basis is that in terms of the development of indigenous companies it would be possible to make use of a significantly larger domestic market, an important requirement – as has been argued – for the development of a strong industrial base. The structuralist arguments referred to earlier show that the small size of a domestic market can act as a major obstacle to the creation of large and internationally competitive companies. While it could be argued that the creation of an integrated market in Europe will help bring this about, it is clear that the political divide in Ireland acts against the full development of economies of scale and scope. In this regard an EC official has said that

'In Denmark the internal sales per capita are twice as high as the combined sales of Northern Ireland and the Republic of Ireland'.[25] An increase in intra-island sales and greater economic integration could, therefore, expand employment substantially.

It is clear that industrial policy is going to remain on the political agenda in Ireland for the immediate future. It is important, therefore, that it is not just the intricacies of policy implementation which are looked at in any further reviews, but that the wider political framework within which industrial policy has to operate is seriously considered. In many ways it is developments at the political level which could have the biggest and most positive impact on the effectiveness of future Irish industrial policy.

Notes

1 O'Malley, E. (1989), *Industry and Economic Development, the Challenge for the Latecomer*, Gill and Macmillan, Dublin.

2 Munck, R. (1993), *The Irish Economy – Results and Prospects*, Pluto Press, London.

3 O'Malley, E. (1981), 'The decline of Irish industry in the nineteenth century', *The Economic and Social Review*, 13, 1.

4 NIEC (1991), *Economic Strategy in Northern Ireland*, Northern Ireland Economic Council, Report 88, Belfast.

5 NIEC (1990), *Economic Assessment: April 1990*, Northern Ireland Economic Council, Report 81, Belfast.

6 Hamilton, D. (1990), 'Industrial development policy in Northern Ireland – an evaluation of the IDB', *The Economic and Social Review*, 22, 1, October.

7 Gudgin, G. *et al.* (1989), *Job Generation in Manufacturing Industry 1973–86*, Northern Ireland Economic Research Centre, Belfast.

8 NESC (1982), *A Review of Industrial Policy*, National Economic and Social Council, No. 64, Dublin, p. 33.

9 Department of Industry and Commerce (1990), *Review of Industrial Performance 1990*, The Stationery Office, Dublin.

10 Culliton, J. (1992), *A Time for Change: Industrial Policy for the 1990s*, Report of the Industrial Policy Review Group, The Stationary Office, Dublin, p. 63.

11 NIEC (1990), *The Private Sector in the Northern Ireland Economy*, Northern Ireland Economic Council, Report 82, Belfast, p. 49.

12 Hamilton, 'Industrial development policy'.

13 NESC (1982), *Review of Industrial Policy*, Report 64, Dublin, p. 185.

14 McMahon, J., McHugh, D. and Bowe, R. (1988), 'The IDA's Annual Survey of the Irish Economy Expenditures of the Manufacturing Sector, Some Insights into Manufacturing Performance', Paper presented to the Irish Economic Association Conference, Carrickmacross, May.

15 NIEC (1992), *Inward Investment in Northern Ireland*, Northern Ireland Economic Council, Report 99, Belfast.

16 NIEC (1990), *The Industrial Development Board for Northern Ireland: Selective Financial Assistance and Economic Development Policy*, Northern Ireland Economic Council, Report 79, Belfast.

17 O'Malley, *Industry and Economic Development*.

18 PESP (1991), *Programme for Economic and Social Progress*, The Stationery Office, Dublin, p. 45.

19 DED (1990), *Competing in the 1990s – The Key to Growth*, Department of Economic Development, HMSO, Belfast.

20 DED (1987), *Building a Stronger Economy, the Pathfinder Process*, Department of Economic Development, HMSO, Belfast, July.

21 NIEC, *Economic Strategy*.

22 NIEC, *Inward Investment*.

23 Hamilton, D. (1993), 'Foreign direct investment and industrial development in Northern Ireland' in Teague, P. (ed.), *The Economy of Northern Ireland – Perspectives for Structural Change*, Lawrence and Wishart, London.

24 Harris, R. I. D. (1987), 'The role of manufacturing in regional growth', *Regional Studies*, 21, 4.

25 European Commission Office in Northern Ireland (1991), 'Fringe Benefits', *Europe in Northern Ireland*, Belfast, July.

7 *Joan Moss*

Agriculture

The agricultural industry is important in both Irish economies. Agriculture, forestry and fishing in Northern Ireland provide employment (both full and part-time) for 44,000 people, which represents almost 8 per cent of the total employment and generates 4 per cent of the Gross Domestic Product. In the Republic, 170,000 people are employed in agriculture, approximately 14.5 per cent of the total work-force, and the agricultural industry accounts for 10.5 per cent of Gross Domestic Product[1] (see Table 7.1).

The output from the two farming sectors is by no means produced solely for local consumption (see Table 7.2). The proportion of Northern Ireland output of the main agricultural products – beef, sheepmeat and milk and dairy products – which are exported ranges from 24 per cent for sheepmeat to 73 per cent for milk and dairy products. The level of self-sufficiency for beef, sheepmeat, cheese and butter in the Republic ranges from 190 per cent for sheepmeat to 765 per cent for beef. It has been estimated that the exports of agricultural and food products account for approximately 20 per cent of Northern Ireland's gross exports (which includes sales to Britain) and 25 per cent of total exports from the Republic comprise agricultural and food products and beverages (see Table 7.1).

Table 7.1 *The agricultural sectors of Northern Ireland and the Republic of Ireland*

	NI	ROI
Number of farm holdings (000)	42	217
Number of full-time holdings (000)	13	69
Farm workforce (000)	44	164
Contribution to:		
total employment (per cent)	7.9	14.5
Gross Domestic Product (per cent)	4.0	10.5
gross exports (per cent)	20.0	25.0

Note
Data refer to 1987 to 1989 depending on source.
Sources: Central Statistical Office, Dublin.
  Department of Agriculture for Northern Ireland.

Table 7.2 *The importance of agricultural exports to Northern Ireland and the Republic of Ireland*

Agricultural products	Proportion of NI output exported[a]	Level of self-sufficiency
beef	62	765
sheepmeat	24	190
milk and dairy products	73	–
cheese		500
butter		479

Note
[a]Level of self-sufficiency not calculated for Northern Ireland.
Sources: EC Commission.
  Department of Agriculture for Northern Ireland.

Farming structures, enterprises and incomes

The structure of the farm sectors in both jurisdictions is very similar, both being dominated by small family-run farms. Of the 42,000 farm holdings in Northern Ireland, only 30,000 operate as farm businesses, with the remainder either wholly or mainly let in conacre or with no recorded farming activity. Only 13,000 (approximately 30 per cent) of the farm businesses are considered large enough to provide full-time employment for at least one person. Of the 217,000 farm holdings in the Republic 69,000 (32 per cent) are classified as full-time farms on a labour requirement basis, i.e. requiring at least 0.75 labour units.

Grazing livestock enterprises, i.e. dairying, beef cattle and sheep production, are the dominant farming enterprises. In 1989, they accounted for 73 per cent and 71 per cent respectively of the gross farming output in Northern Ireland and the Republic. Since accession to the EC in 1973, there have been very similar changes in the structure of agricultural production in Northern Ireland and the Republic of Ireland. While the number of farms which had dairy cows, beef cattle or pigs declined throughout the 1980s, the average size of dairying, beef and pig enterprises increased. Sheep production, however, experienced a dramatic expansion, particularly towards the end of the 1980s, in both the number of farms with sheep and the average size of flock.

Net farm income is total enterprise output less total inputs. It represents the return to the farmer and spouse for their manual and managerial labour and tenant type capital (i.e. livestock, crops and machinery but excluding land and buildings).[2] Official estimates of net farm income in Northern Ireland and family farm incomes in the Republic of Ireland are calculated using different definitions of farm population. A larger number of smaller farms are included in the Republic's estimates. Consequently, direct comparisons between the two are difficult to interpret. A further complication arises when considering the average farm incomes because of the wide variation in incomes arising from differing farm business sizes and types of farming enterprises. Some similar broad trends in farming income, however, can be deduced for the two parts of Ireland over recent years:[3]

- farming incomes vary considerably from year to year, reflecting external factors such as weather conditions;
- average farming incomes, which were depressed at the beginning of the 1980s, recovered substantially until the middle of the decade when extremely severe weather conditions caused farming incomes to fall;
- for most of the 1980s average net farm income was less than the average total personal income for those employed in the non-farm sectors;
- at the end of the 1980s and early 1990s there was another sharp fall in farming income;
- incomes from dairying were consistently higher than those from other livestock enterprises; and incomes from cropping were the most variable from year to year.

Farming incomes are forecast to remain under pressure for the foreseeable future. For many farming households, particularly where the farm is small, income from off-farm employment and transfers (e.g. welfare payments, state pensions) account for more than half of total farm household income.

Government and EC intervention in agriculture

Throughout the world governments intervene in the agricultural sector. The following reasons are often given:

1 Market price instability – a high degree of variability in the volume of agricultural output from year to year causes price instability. The main reasons for output variability are weather, incidence of animal and plant pests and diseases and the tendency for concerted production decisions by a large number of farmers to lead to over- or under-supply.

2   Downward trend in farm incomes – modern technology
     has increased the productivity of farm labour in an era
     when demand for food is fairly static in the developed
     world. Agricultural labour has not been sufficiently mobile
     to leave farming in necessary numbers. Consequently, too
     many people are trying to obtain a living from agriculture
     and this pushes down the individual incomes.
3   Security and stability of supply – governments wish to
     ensure that in times of international emergency there are
     adequate and secure stocks of food. (The experiences of
     food shortages in Western Europe during the Second
     World War have led to great importance being attached
     to a high degree of self-sufficiency in food production.)
4   Price of food – a relatively high proportion of consumer
     expenditure (typically between 15 and 25 per cent) goes
     on food and beverages, depending on the income level
     of consumers. At very low levels of income, an even
     higher proportion of income is spent on food. There are,
     consequently, strong welfare arguments for keeping down
     the cost of food.
5   Consumer protection – governments acknowledge the
     importance of ensuring that consumers are protected by
     specifying standards of food quality.

The Common Agricultural Policy of the European Community

The European Economic Community was established by
the Treaty of Rome in 1957. Article 39.1 of the Treaty
identified the objectives for 'a common policy in the sphere
of agriculture':

(a) to increase agricultural productivity by promoting technical
    progress and by ensuring the rational development of
    agricultural production and the optimum utilisation of the
    factors of production, in particular labour;

(b) thus, to ensure a fair standard of living for the agricultural community, in particular by increasing the individual earnings of persons engaged in agriculture;

(c) to stabilise markets;

(d) to assure the availability of supplies; and

(e) to ensure that supplies reach consumers at reasonable prices.

The CAP as such did not come into existence until the mid-1960s. There are two main elements in the CAP: structural measures and price and market support. Both are financed by the European Agricultural Guidance and Guarantee Fund (EAGGF). Structural policies are designed to tackle the fundamental structural problems of the agricultural sectors of the community, and the price and market policies are concerned with the market alleviation of the adverse consequences of the structural problems, mainly low prices and incomes. It was originally intended that CAP resources would be divided approximately 25/75 per cent between structural measures and price and market support. At the time of the United Kingdom's and the Republic of Ireland's accession to the EC, only 5 per cent of CAP spending was devoted to structural measures. At the same time, more than two-thirds of the EC budget was devoted to the CAP. In 1990, structural measures accounted for 8.5 per cent of CAP expenditure and the CAP accounted for 58 per cent of the EC budget.[4]

Price and market policies

The price and market policies of the CAP are based on three fundamental principles:

1   unity of the market – gradual harmonisation of farm prices in member states;

2   community preference – creation of a customs union whereby trade with fellow member states is given preference compared with trade with third countries. This entails protectionism

whereby exports from the Community are subsidised and imports into the Community taxed;

3   financial solidarity – establishment of the European Agricultural Guidance and Guarantee Fund, whereby expenses incurred as a result of the CAP are financed by the Community and income generated by the CAP is regarded as part of the income (own resources) of the Community.

It must be emphasized that a producer's income has to be determined principally by the price his produce fetches in the market rather than by direct income supplements or allowances determined by area of crops grown or livestock numbers. Prices are determined by markets within the framework of the CAP regimes at a level which is designed to ensure that even relatively high-cost producers can earn a living. Differing terminology is used for different commodities but the underlying price support principle is the same.

A desired market price for Community producers is determined annually for each commodity. This is called the Target, Base or Guide price depending on the commodity. Once this reference point has been agreed two additional prices can be determined for each commodity.

(a) Threshold price – the minimum entry price chargeable by importers from third countries. Since imports are free to enter at prices above the threshold price, this effectively establishes a ceiling on EC internal market prices.

(b) Intervention (or buying-in) price – the floor price at which national intervention agencies are obliged to purchase Community produce offered to them (for those products covered by intervention support). The intervention price is set significantly higher than the world price. Consequently, market prices for each commodity are kept above world prices.

The mechanisms which enforce price support and control the flow of imports into and subsidise the flow of exports out of

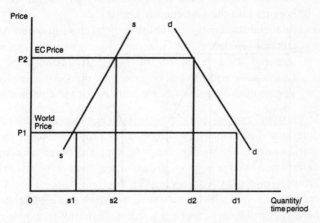

Figure 7.1 Price support mechanism when the European Community is net importer.

the Community (thereby supporting the incomes of Community farmers and exercising Community preference) can be explained by a simple economic model (following an analysis of EC price support established by Josling in 1969).[5]

In Figures 7.1 and 7.2 ss is the supply schedule and dd the demand schedule for community producers and consumers respectively. When the Community is a net importer of a product (see Figure 7.1), and the world price P1 'rules' in the Community, 0s1 would be produced within the Community and 0d1 would be consumed, hence d1 – s1 would be imported. With the internal EC price set at the higher level P2, 0s2 is produced within the Community and 0d2 consumed. Consequently the volume of imports is reduced and the degree of self-sufficiency increased. More resources are employed to produce the commodity with the supported price than if the world price ruled. There is also an overall reduction in consumption levels.

The EC price is maintained above the level of world prices by imposing taxes (levies) on imports, whereby the difference

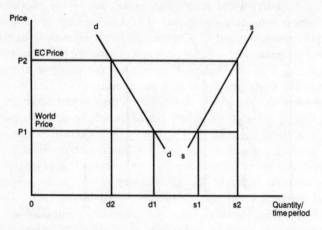

Figure 7.2   Price support mechanism when the European Community is net exporter.

between the prices has to be forfeited by the importer. If the Community is more than self-sufficient in a commodity then other policy mechanisms are necessary to ensure that producers obtain the high EC price.

When the Community is a net exporter of a commodity (see Figure 7.2), if the world price P1 pertained in the Community 0s1 would be produced and 0d1 consumed, therefore, 0s1 – 0d1 would be exported. At the higher EC price of P2, production is at the higher level, 0s2, and consumption is reduced to 0d2 and there is a surplus 0s2 – 0d2. Intervention buying is the primary internal market price support mechanism for commodities in surplus. However, intervention stocks cannot be held indefinitely, and even if they could, the storage costs have to be considered. This raises the issue of what is to become of intervention stocks. Much has to be exported on to the world market and experience has shown that it is less costly (in EC budgetary terms) for traders to export commodities directly than to go through intervention.

Exports, however, cannot be expected to be sold at more

than the lower world price. The answer lies in the provision of export refunds (restitutions). The EC exporter is paid an export restitution out of Community funds equivalent to the price differential P2 – P1 for each unit of exported produce. The increased level of subsidised exports has the effect of driving down the world price; this is to the detriment of Third World exporters who are widely dependent on their export revenues.

This is a highly simplified exposition of the price support system for a commodity. There may be additional payments to producers which are not linked to world market prices, e.g. direct aids in the form of headage payments in less advantaged regions. To highlight the complexities of the price support and market control mechanisms employed in the CAP there follows a brief review of the three commodity regimes of most importance to Northern Ireland and the Republic of Ireland, i.e. for dairy products, beef and veal and sheepmeat.

The milk regime

This regime, which covers a range of milk products as well as fresh or preserved milk and cream, came into operation in 1968. It had two major objectives: to ensure a reasonable income for milk producers and to stabilise markets by balancing supply and demand. These objectives have been difficult to achieve. In 1968, the average herd size in the Community was less than eight cows and so in order to secure a satisfactory level of income across the EC the target price was set at a high level. Consequently, price support has proved expensive and at the time of Northern Ireland's and the Republic of Ireland's accession accounted for almost 40 per cent of the total expenditure of the Guarantee Sector of FEOGA (European Agricultural Guarantee and Guidance Fund), even though milk production represented only 18.5 per cent of the Community's final agricultural production. The high level of support for the dairy sector stimulated milk production in many member states. The increase in production between 1973 and

1983 was 58 and 70 per cent in Northern Ireland and the Republic of Ireland respectively. Dairying has continued to remain consistently the most profitable grassland-based farm enterprise in Northern Ireland and the Republic of Ireland and dairy products constitute a major proportion of agricultural exports from both Northern Ireland and the Republic of Ireland (see Table 7.2).

Numerous schemes designed to increase milk and milk product consumption and reduce production have been introduced, thereby complicating the milk regime. The underlying objective of the Community policy for dairying is the management of markets for dairy products so that milk producers obtain the target price for their milk. The price of milk is supported by intervention buying of certain milk products, and until 1987, intervention agencies were obliged to purchase any butter or skimmed-milk powder (SMP) offered to them. The increase in milk production, however, was not being matched by increasing consumption of milk products and consequently intervention stocks grew to unacceptably high levels. Since then, limits have been placed on intervention purchases, unless the market price in a region or a member state falls below approximately 90 per cent of the intervention price.

Measures to reduce supply

The co-responsibility levy was introduced in 1977. This levy on the products of milk is a percentage of the target price and was designed to create and finance various market expansion measures and help fund the disposal of products which were in surplus. The co-responsibility levy had little effect in reducing milk production and a more drastic measure, milk quota, was introduced.

In 1984 a supplementary levy (the Superlevy), designed to make surplus milk production uneconomic, was introduced, initially for five years, and was charged on all milk produced above a certain reference quantity (the milk quota). member states were allocated a quota which equalled the quantity which had been delivered to dairies in 1981 plus an additional 1 per cent. Despite the introduction of quotas surpluses continued to grow and by 1986 quotas were further reduced by 3 per cent. Since then a further 5.5 per cent reduction in quota has occurred.

The Community Outgoers Scheme (COS), introduced in 1987–8, was designed to compensate dairy farmers who voluntarily relinquished their quota, thereby avoiding the imposition of compulsory quota cuts on all producers. The uptake fell far short of desired levels and further compulsory quota cuts had to be implemented.

Measures to increase demand

A wide variety of measures designed to increase the demand for milk have been introduced over the years. Disposal schemes for skim milk have operated to subsidise the use of SMP and liquid skim milk fed to calves. Short-term schemes have offered butter to consumers at highly subsidised rates, e.g. Christmas butter, but these schemes are very expensive to operate and the substitution by consumers of subsidised butter for unsubsidised is very high. There have also been schemes to supply butter to the food industry and to non-profit making organisations.

The external regime

As described in earlier sections, the difference between the world prices and the threshold prices for milk products determines the magnitude of the levies imposed on milk product imports, thereby ensuring that these cannot undercut the target price in the EC; Export refund guarantees are granted on sales of milk products to countries outside the EC, which cover the difference between the internal price for milk products and prices in international trade.

Despite the lowering of milk production levels in the EC,

the milk regime remains the most expensive commodity regime in the CAP. Aggregate consumption levels continue to decline and large surpluses, which are very expensive to store and subsequently dispose of, still exist. Consequently, quotas are likely to remain with further reductions being implemented. The continuing disproportionate support for dairying could lead to further real falls in the milk price, as a result of pressures both from within the EC and internationally as a result of trade negotiations.

The beef and veal regime

The beef regime covers live cattle and calves and a wide range of beef products, whether fresh, chilled, frozen, salted, dried or smoked. It is worth noting that beef production is the second largest element in total agricultural production in the EC; this is also reflected in its contribution to gross agricultural output and agricultural exports in both Northern Ireland and the Republic of Ireland. Although the EC was a net importer of beef when the regime was introduced in 1968 it has been a net exporter since 1979, reflecting an increase in degree of self-sufficiency in common with most major commodities.

The internal regime

As with other common policies, the support measures for the beef regime are based on Guide and Intervention prices set annually. The intervention system introduced in 1972 was intended to act as a market of last resort; however, it quickly became the major support mechanism in the beef regime. In 1981–82 it was decided to place restrictions on intervention buying and in 1987 and again in 1989 further restrictions were imposed.

Because of these restrictions there is a 'safety net' buying mechanism available to prevent market collapse. The intervention buying of beef has a major drawback, when compared to intervention buying of other commodities. Beef must be frozen and so it automatically drops in value and the uses to which it can be put are limited. In addition, the cost of storing frozen beef is very high.

There is an Aids to Private Storage Scheme available to support the market without beef being bought into intervention. A subsidy for storage aid is paid to the owner of the meat to hold it off the market for a limited period of time. This form of market support is more flexible and cheaper than intervention, and because the meat is privately owned it is generally better cared for than meat in public storage.

Throughout the 1980s there was a shift in support away from intervention buying to the payment of various premia to farmers. Payments were made on cattle at six months, suckler cows (where it could be shown that the farmer obtained more than half his income from farming and spent more than half his time on the farm) and on male cattle over six months of age. In addition, Hill Livestock Compensatory Amounts, described in more detail in the section on structural measures, are also paid.

The external regime

All cattle and beef imports into the EC are subject to customs duties at various rates and from time to time variable import levies are imposed. There are, however, a number of concessionary import schemes from certain Third World countries whereby predetermined volumes of beef imports are permitted duty-free with minimal import levies imposed. Furthermore, by agreement through GATT, specific volumes of beef are imported subject only to customs duty. Exports of beef from the EC attract export restitutions (subsidies) to compensate for the shortfall in price obtained on the world market compared with the higher administered prices pertaining within the Community. These restitutions are of particular importance to Northern Ireland and the Republic of Ireland, which are both net exporters of beef.

The sheepmeat regime

At the outset the EC did not have a common sheepmeat policy as France was the only original member with a significant sheepmeat sector. This situation changed with the accession of the United Kingdom and the Republic of Ireland, both major lamb producers and consumers, in 1973. During their transitional period member states continued with their national support measures for sheepmeat. In 1977, however, the Irish Government brought France to the European Court of Justice for violating the Treaty of Rome by banning imports of Irish lamb. France traditionally had intensive sheepmeat production with high costs and highly supported prices and feared the competition from member states who produced lamb by extensive low-cost systems. Consequently an agreement was reached whereby the Republic of Ireland was permitted to export a given volume of lamb to France each week. Northern Ireland farmers benefited from this arrangement as they could easily take their sheep to the Republic of Ireland for onward shipment to France. The United Kingdom, still barred from the French market, contested the bilateral agreement. Finally, in 1980, a common sheepmeat regime was introduced.

The internal regime

The common sheepmeat regime, which is quite different from other CAP regimes, covers sheep and goat products with the exception of wool, which is defined as an industrial product. The organisation of the internal sheepmeat market is based on:

(a) intervention or deficiency payment (depending on the member state);
(b) a system of premia based on payments per ewe and paid directly to producers.

In order to reduce the smuggling of lamb between Northern Ireland and the Republic of Ireland, Northern Ireland, unlike the rest of the UK, was fully integrated into the intervention and support methods applied in the Republic of Ireland and the rest of the EC, although intervention has never been resorted to in either Northern Ireland or the Republic of Ireland. As a result of the rapid expansion of the Community sheep flock and the consequential increase in the costs of the sheepmeat regime, a Budgetary Stabiliser mechanism was activated in 1988. Every 1 per cent increase above the threshold flock results in a 1 per cent increase above the decrease in the basic price and consequently a reduction in Ewe Premium paid. At the beginning of 1990 a radical reform of the sheepmeat regime commenced, with the objective of achieving a uniform market support system throughout the EC. Intervention purchase has been removed and replaced by an expanded system of Aids to Private Storage. From 1993 the Ewe Premium is calculated on a community-wide basis. This tends to disadvantage Ireland as the market price here is relatively low by EC standard.

The external regime

When the common sheepmeat regime was introduced a system of Voluntary Restraint Agreements (VRAs) was negotiated whereby world sheepmeat exporters, with New Zealand being most important, agreed to limit their exports to the EC to certain negotiated amounts. Both the Republic of Ireland and France were initially designated sensitive areas, with curtailments placed on sheepmeat imports into these member states. In the negotiation of the VRAs the EC agreed not to export subsidised sheepmeat in excess of traditional levels, and consequently virtually no sheepmeat is exported from the EC.

The agrimonetary system

This is a rather complex system and the explanation given below is the briefest of outlines. In converting the mutually agreed guide prices which are set annually for agricultural products into the national currencies of the member states, problems arose if there were changes in the exchange rates between the currencies of the member states, which are determined in the money markets. If a currency depreciated in value this led to the farmers who operated in that currency receiving a higher price (in terms of their own currency) for their produce whereas farmers in other member states with appreciating currencies would see a decline (in terms of their currencies) in their prices. This was seen to be politically unacceptable.

To overcome this difficulty, and at the same time insulate consumers from the effects of market exchange-rate adjustments on food prices, a system of green rates was introduced. These rates were used to convert the guide prices into national currencies. Compensatory payments known as Monetary Compensatory Amounts (MCAs) are also made at frontiers to prevent intra-EC trade distortions, where green rates and market rates diverge.

When a member state has a currency which is depreciating relative to other EC currencies, this gives scope for green rate devaluations which would provide the farmers in that state with higher agricultural product prices. This has occurred even at times when the guide prices, as expressed in European Currency Units, remained constant. The main problem which arose because of the operation of the agrimonetary system within the island of Ireland was the considerable incentive it provided to smuggle cattle, pigs and grain. With the prospect of the completion of the internal market and closer monetary union, the European Commission aims to have MCAs eliminated.

Structural policy and rural development

As indicated earlier, the two main arms of the CAP are price and market support and structural measures. Although structural policy addresses the underlying problems of EC farming rather than treating the symptoms, it has consistently accounted for a minor share of CAP expenditure. The structural difficulties can be summarised in economic terms as the misallocation of resources, whereby too many people and too much capital and land are employed in the agricultural sector. Consequently, too many people are trying to earn a living solely from farming and this is reflected in large numbers of small holdings and low per capita income.

The two main elements of structural policy are:

1 measures directed at decreasing the numbers of people employed in agriculture;
2 measures directed at increasing farm size.

The early CAP structural measures were designed with the objective of improving the structure of the agricultural sector by the modernising and enlarging of holdings; training labour and encouraging the exit of excess, particularly elderly, labour from agriculture; the strengthening of processing and marketing structures, and the reduction of structural handicaps and the improvement of infrastructure in specific regions.

Initially it was felt that by modernising, i.e. investing in modern technology and farming methods, farmers would increase their levels of output and hence their incomes. This course of action usually resulted in an increasing degree of specialisation on farms. Capital grants were available for farm businesses capable of generating a target income per labour unit (set at a level comparable with non-farming incomes) on completion of a farm plan. The farm modernisation initiatives had a substantial uptake and farm output expanded rapidly, encouraged by the high levels of guaranteed prices. Concurrently, financial incentives were available for those taking early retirement from farming whose land would be amalgamated with other land to form viable farm units. This initiative generated a limited response as it was felt that the financial incentives were not sufficiently large. Farming families were also given access to socio-economic guidance, the first recognition that the financial well-being of the farming family might entail looking outside the agricultural sector for employment opportunities.

The other structural measure with considerable impact on farming incomes in the 1970s was the introduction of differentially larger grants and headage payments for breeding cattle and sheep in the designated Less Favoured Areas (LFA). Most farmers considered the headage payments (Hill Livestock Compensatory Allowances) to be part of price support policy but they were in fact an important regional element of structural policy. They were designed as direct income payments to help farmers to remain in the LFA, despite their production and marketing disadvantages. By 1990 approximately 75 per cent of Northern Ireland and 50 per cent of the Republic of Ireland were designated as LFA.

By the mid-1980s it was recognised that the rate of expansion of output, compared with internal consumption, could not be permitted to continue indefinitely as it was generating ever-increasing surpluses and associated escalating budgetary costs. There was also pressure for reduction of protectionism of agriculture via reduced price support coming from the Uruguay round of GATT negotiations on trade reform. It was also recognised that despite all the intervention in agricultural markets, there still existed a serious low income problem for smaller farmers. As support was linked to production, the larger farmers, while only accounting for 20 per cent of holdings, generated 80 per cent of production and hence gained 80 per cent of support.[6]

It was envisaged that in future market forces would have to be more important in determining levels of farm output and price restraint was introduced. It was considered no longer feasible to provide assistance to farmers to improve their farming incomes by modernising their farm businesses, if this entailed expanding output of those products in surplus. From 1985 onwards a number of measures were introduced which sought to: improve working conditions on farms; reduce costs; improve the quality of farm produce; and protect and, where possible, enhance the rural environment without increasing farm output.[7]

In a document entitled *The Future of Rural Society*, the European Commission acknowledged that the problems faced by the farming community could not be resolved solely within the agricultural sector.[8] New economic activities were required on and off the farms to stimulate the economies of rural areas. There was also the prospect of the Single European Act coming into force at the end of 1992 and the recognition that disadvantaged peripheral regions might require additional assistance. This led to major reform of the three structural funds of the EC: the Guidance Section of the European Agricultural Guidance and Guarantee Fund; the European Social Fund, which grants aid for training and retraining workers; and the European Regional Development Fund, which has as its objective the encouragement of productive investments and improvement of infrastructures such as roads and telecommunications which assist economies in development.

Rural development is an umbrella term which covers a range of issues, prominent among which are the following: enhancement of economic activity in rural areas; preservation of rural society; preservation of the natural environment; integrating bottom-up and top-down approaches to development; generating partnership between statutory agencies and local groups. The improvement of the structure of the agricultural sector is seen as essential for rural development.

The structural policy reforms entail an increase in structural funds expenditure and a concentration of the activities of the funds on five priority objectives, the first of which concerns Northern Ireland and the Republic of Ireland. Objective One is the development and structural adjustment of the regions whose development is lagging behind (defined by per capita GDP being less than 75 per cent of the Community average). This is the highest priority category of disadvantaged regions and will attract the greatest increase in structural funding. The Republic of Ireland qualified as an Objective One region and Northern Ireland was also granted Objective One status, although qualifying not strictly on GDP per capita grounds, but because of particular development difficulties.[9]

A range of initiatives is encouraged including measures to maintain the countryside, reorganise and strengthen agricultural structures and assist rural areas. There is an emphasis on diversification, especially those providing alternative incomes for farmers; encouragement for tourism and development of crafts; protection of the environment and the countryside; development and exploitation of woodlands, and agricultural vocational training. There has to be a partnership whereby funding comes from the Community, the member state, and private sources. Since all disadvantaged regions face unique difficulties and have individual strengths, in terms of resources available for development and market opportunities, there is no attempt to introduce a uniform rural development initiative across the Community. Development plans have to be tailored to the needs of each disadvantaged region. The rural development initiative has four stages:

1   Member s ate draws up development plan;
2   European Commission consequently decides on a Community Support Framework;
3   the development plan, tailored to regional requirements, is implemented;
4   monitoring of development plan.

The focus is on bringing together the ideas and aspirations of the people in a region and the expertise and planning skills available at the national and Community levels. This is known as a bottom-up-top-down-approach. Development plans covering the period 1989 to 1993 have been enacted for both Northern Ireland and the Republic of Ireland, but it is too early to assess their impact. The Community's contribution to these plans amounts to approximately 0.8 and 3.6 billion ECU respectively, with total financing of 1.8 and 8.4 billion ECU. The remainder will come from national exchequers and locally raised funds.

Reform of the CAP

It is now widely recognised that the CAP has been too successful in stimulating food supply and the status quo cannot continue. The internal EC problems with the CAP which necessitate reform are as follows:

1   surpluses stimulated by price guarantees directly linked to production – between 1978 and 1988 EC production increased by 2 per cent per annum while internal consumption grew by 0.5 per cent per annum. Consequently there is a severe misallocation of resources, with resources used in agricultural production which could be more efficiently deployed in other sectors;

2   excessive Intervention Stocks – by mid-1991 surplus stocks, which are costly to store, were valued at 3.7 billion ECU and amounted to approximately 20 million tonnes of cereals, 1 million tonnes of dairy products and 750,000 tonnes of beef;

3   escalating budgetary expenditure on support measures, intervention stocks and subsidies for exports dumped on to the over-supplied world market. The annual EC Agricultural Budget increased from approximately 15 billion ECUs in 1983 to 30 billion ECUs in 1991;

4   inbuilt incentives to greater farming intensity and ever higher production putting the environment at risk;

5   the welfare equity issue – the majority of expenditure goes to a minority of larger farmers mainly in northern EC countries, despite the low-income problems of the smaller farmers, predominantly in the southern regions;

6   the onerous burden placed on EC taxpayers and consumers comprising the costs of support and artificially high food prices.

In addition to these internal problems there are world equity issues associated with the detrimental effects of EC dumping on the world market and the consequent decline in the export revenues of Third World countries. There is also pressure emanating from the GATT negotiations, which are pursuing the liberalisation of international trade. Although strictly a separate issue, a key element in the negotiations is the discussion on the level of reduction in the EC agricultural protection which is acceptable to all parties.

The European Commission's proposals for reform were widely debated and an agreement was eventually reached in mid-1992. The main features of the reforms are as follows:

- major reduction in prices, e.g. cereals −29 per cent, butter −5 per cent, beef −15 per cent. These will lead to corresponding reductions in the prices for pigmeat, poultrymeat and eggs;
- substantial compensatory premia for price reductions;
- a range of supply control measures including set-aside in cereals, quotas for suckler cows and sheep, upper limits on number of livestock eligible for compensatory premia;
- extensification premia to encourage less intense use of land for beef production; deseasonalisation premia to encourage a more even pattern of cattle slaughter throughout the year;
- a focus on support of small farmers by exempting them from cereals set-aside requirements and the maximum limits placed on number of beef cattle and sheep eligible for premia.[10]

There are also accompanying measures concerning environmentally-friendly farming methods, afforestation of agricultural land, and early retirement of farmers (in the Republic of Ireland but not in Northern Ireland).

Impact of CAP reforms

It is difficult to predict accurately the short and longer term impact of CAP reform for Northern Ireland and the Republic of Ireland until the fine details are released. The short-term impact associated with existing farm production patterns will concern: changes in farming income at both the sectoral and individual farm level influenced by the extent to which compensatory payments substitute for reduced returns from the market; employment (both on and off-farm); consumer benefits (via cheaper food); budgetary expenditure and the environment.

A reformed CAP regime will affect the relative profitability of different production systems and the competitiveness of Northern Ireland and the Republic of Ireland farming *vis-à-vis* other member states of the EC and the rest of the world. Consequently new production patterns will emerge before the longer term impact becomes discernible. It would appear that the reforms will not save budgetary expenditure and could increase it, particularly in the early years. The expenditure will be redirected away from larger farms towards smaller farms. In addition, mainly because of the predominance of grazing livestock enterprises and the high proportion of farm output exported, the farming sectors in Northern Ireland and the Republic of Ireland could incur a decline in income and employment, despite the incidence of small farms in both regions eligible for a high level of compensation. These losses could exceed any financial or employment benefits accruing to the rest of their economies. Furthermore, the losses would be borne most heavily by larger farmers and those with the most intensive farming systems.

It is because of the prospect of such changes that rural development initiatives have gained such a high priority in the minds of policy makers. With the farming sectors providing less employment for the rural populations in the future, alternative/additional forms of employment will have to be secured if the rural society is to be stabilised and out-migration halted before irreversible change is inflicted.

Notes

1 It should be noted that the employment figures are not directly comparable owing to different methods of data collection. An equivalent Northern Ireland figure to that for the Republic of Ireland would be approximately 30,000.

2   Family farm income is the value of gross output of the farm (including headage payments) less total expenses. It represents the return to the factors of production (land, labour, management and capital) employed in the farm business.

3   Moss, J. E., Phelan, J. F., McHenry, H. L., Caskie, D. P., Markey, A. P. (1991), *Study of Farm Incomes in Northern Ireland and the Republic of Ireland*, Co-operation North, Third Study Series, Report No. 1.

4   Commission of the European Communities (1990), *The Agricultural Situation in the Community*, CM58/90.

5   Josling, T. E. (1969), 'A formal approach to agricultural policy', *Journal of Agricultural Economics*, 20.

6   Commission of the European Communities (1990), Green Paper, *Restoring Equilibrium on the Agricultural Markets*, 3/90.

7   Commission of the European Communities (1985), Green Paper, *Perspectives for the Common Agricultural Policy*, 33/85.

8   Commission of the European Communities (1988), *The Future of Rural Society*, Bulletin of the European Community Supplement, 4/88, Commission communication to Parliament and the Council.

9   Commission of the European Communities (1990), Green Paper, *Agriculture and the Reform of the Structural Funds – Vade Mecum*, 5/90.

10 Commission of the European Communities (1991), *The Development and the Future of the Common Agricultural Policy*, COM (91)258.

References

Department of Agriculture for Northern Ireland, *Statistical Review of Northern Ireland Agriculture*, various years.

Central Statistics Office, *EC Farm Structures Surveys*, Dublin, various years.

8 *Leslie Carswell*
Health policy

Health and social services are key areas of social policy in developed countries. There is a continuing concern as the costs of these services are burgeoning, demand from a more aware and articulate public is rising but the resources to meet these are under severe strain from competing areas of expenditure. All these factors are relevant in the two Irish jurisdictions. In each, health and social services absorb significant shares of resources, especially when both parts of the island are regarded as having low per capita income.

The debate on health services extends beyond considerations of finance. The health of the population is influenced by its environment, life style, education and housing. In Ireland as a whole the health status of the population compares well with that of other parts of the EC, and with the exception of diseases of the circulatory system, Ireland enjoys relatively reasonable health (see Table 8.1).

This chapter will concentrate on aspects of the health services, and their related personal social services or community care systems. For simplicity the term 'health' is used to refer to both health and personal social services. Professionals in the personal social services in Northern Ireland or the community care programme in the Republic are wary of being grouped with health. Their reservations about the medical model of health will be outlined later in this chapter. The main divisions of the analysis presented here are:

Table 8.1 *Health status in the Republic and Northern Ireland*

	Crude death rate per 100,000		Cancer death		Disease of circulatory system		Respiratory TB	
	M	F	M	F	M	F	M	F
Highest other EC country	1192[1]	1140[3]	324[4]	278[6]	540[7]	607[8]	4.6[5]	1.4[10]
The Republic of Ireland	961	824	219	184	452	393	1.9	1.2
Northern Ireland	998	950	224	205	484	481	0.9	0.7
Lowest other EC country	842[2]	722[2]	191[5]	135[2]	332[2]	367[2]	0.2[9]	0.00[11]

Notes

1. Belgium (Scotland 1230)
2. Spain
3. Germany (FR) (Scotland 1197)
4. Belgium
5. Portugal
6. Denmark
7. Denmark (Scotland 598)
8. Germany (FR) (Scotland 616)
9. Netherlands
10. Greece
11. Luxembourg

Source: Adopted from Health Statistics 1990, Department of Health, Dublin Stationery Office.

(a) health needs and status;
(b) administrative structures;
(c) funding;
(d) pressures for change.

Health needs and status

Obviously the size and make-up of the population has an important bearing on total health needs. The two parts of the island both display similar characteristics in that they have a relatively young population and a smaller proportion of elderly people compared with many European countries. Over half of the Republic's 3.5 million population are under thirty, while a quarter of Northern Ireland's 1.6 million are children under fifteen years old (see Table 8.2). In addition, there has been a drift of population to the conurbations around Belfast and Dublin. The consequences are that there are large rural areas which are sparsely populated, often with elderly people.

These demographic projections suggest that serious imbalances are likely to persist. Over the next ten years, the greatest percentage increase is expected to be in those over sixty-five. For example, in Northern Ireland this group will increase by 6.5 per cent while the group of those aged less than fifteen will increase only by 1.7 per cent. This changing age structure has obvious implications for the future; more elderly people will require care but there will be relatively fewer younger people to provide it. While most people retain a capacity for independent living well past retirement age, a minority will eventually need some form of continuing care. If this involves only general care assistance, it need not be expensive. A separate but related trend is for more sophisticated and costly treatment, such as hip joint replacement, to be offered to older people. Expensive operations, which were once available only to the young, are being carried out more generally. The associated increase in costs is falling on a smaller taxable population. Another area of increasing burden for the health services is the fifty to sixty

Table 8.2 *Population in the Republic and Northern Ireland: main characteristics*

	Republic 1991	Northern Ireland 1991	Other EC 1989
Total	3,523,401	1,577,836	320,222,700
Age groups			
0–14	962,758 (27%)	385,275 (24%)	Highest 22% (Portugal) Lowest 15% (France)
65 and over	394,830 (11%)	199,054 (13%)	Highest 16% (Denmark) Lowest 13% (Portugal)
Dependency ratio[a]	63	59	Highest 52% (Portugal) Lowest 43% (German FR)
Density	51	112	Highest 360 (Netherlands) Lowest 76 (Greece)

Notes

[a] The number of persons aged 0–14 years and 65 years or over as a percentage of those aged 15–64 years.

Sources: Central Statistics Office, Dublin; Department of Health and Social Services, Belfast.

age group, which often requires expensive surgical treatment, for example, intestinal and cardiac surgery.

When one examines indicators of social need such as levels of deprivation, unemployment rates, average household size and average weekly income, the two parts of the island display a more disadvantaged population compared with Britain and many other parts of Europe. These areas of social welfare policy have proved difficult to tackle. Unemployment is a key indicator of sickness and makes high demands on the caring services.

Infant mortality has always been recognised as a good indicator of the health of a population. Between 1976 and 1990, it fell from 18.3 per 1,000 live births to 7.5 in Northern Ireland. The infant mortality rate improved more than in any other region in the UK in the 1970s and 1980s. Similar figures for the Republic show a fall in the rate from 10 to 8 between the years 1983 and 1989.[1] Undoubtedly improvements in social and environmental conditions as well as better antenatal care have contributed to this decline.

Life expectancy for men and women is the same throughout Ireland. At present it is seventy-seven years for women and seventy-one for men. This represents a substantial improvement since the turn of the century when the corresponding figures were forty-seven for both men and women. Very little change in the survival rate has occurred for people who have reached sixty-five years already, despite improvements in living standards, public hygiene and medical care.

As medical technology advances, there is an increasing potential for the quality of life to improve. Many countries, including the UK and the Republic, subscribe to the World Health Organisation's Health For All initiative. For EC countries, the initiative's aims are:

- to secure equity in health, by reducing the present gap in health status between and within countries;
- to add life to years, by ensuring the full development and use of people's capacity to enjoy life;
- to add health to life, by reducing disease and disability;

- to add years to life, by reducing premature death and increasing life expectancy.

The journey to this future is partly conditioned by the starting point. The origins of the public health care systems in Ireland pre-date partition. However, the services have been transformed especially since 1945, and health status has dramatically improved. The differing systems in Northern Ireland and the Republic have evolved with their own mixture of legislation, governmental influence, timing and, significantly, public and private health provision. Despite the common roots and the implicit direction of the services articulated in the 'Health For All' objectives, there has not been a close relationship or interaction between service providers in the two parts of the island.

One of the major variations between Northern Ireland and the Republic is the differing involvement of the public and private sectors. Another equally important difference is in the level of funding. Both of these issues are addressed below.

Administrative structures

In the Republic, major decisions on health policy and the initiation of health legislation rests with the government. The acts passed by the Oireachtas which govern the provision of the health services do not lay down in detail how services will operate. This is left to regulations made by the Minister for Health, guidelines and directives issued by the Department of Health and to the decisions of the health boards and other executive agencies. The role of the Minister is to see that the health care system operates to the best effect and in accordance with legislation and government policy.

Although the same principles apply in Northern Ireland, a significant difference arises as a result of its constitutional position. Northern Ireland's health services are not fully integrated into the UK National Health Service (NHS). This means that legislation affecting health is passed in Westminster only when Northern Ireland business is being discussed. The government minister responsible for the services is the Secretary of State for Northern Ireland. He is supported by Parliamentary Under-Secretaries of State, one of whom has the health and social services brief. In effect, he is the local minister who is politically accountable to the UK Parliament for the running of the service in Northern Ireland. Local health managers and civil servants are accountable to the minister.

Health policy and health services in Ireland are shaped by past events and developments. Particularly in the Republic, the complex interplay of 'public' and 'private' care in today's health-care system to an extent reflects historical patterns. The complex structure of hospital provision is being influenced by the continuing significance of the private and voluntary hospitals. It has been difficult to rationalise and co-ordinate hospital provision because of the considerable economic and political significance of local health-care institutions from the time of Poor Law Workhouses. Another factor in the evolution of the health-care system has been the recurrent conflict over the appropriate roles of the state, the church and the voluntary sector. One outcome of this is a complex system of entitlement and provision. Out of the 107 acute hospitals, thirty are classified as public voluntary with a variety of origins, often religious. Despite this, they are funded almost entirely by the Department of Health. There are a further 18 private hospitals that get no state funding.

A good place to begin to examine the modern-day history of health and social services in Northern Ireland is the early 1970s. Reorganisation of health coincided with civil unrest. To a large degree the latter resulted in the removal of social services from local council control. As a result, social services were amalgamated with health under a new integrated board structure. This was, and still is, in sharp contrast to the rest of the UK where social services remain under local authority control, organisationally separate from the health authority structure.

The Northern Irish Government department which has responsibility for the combined health and social services is now named the Department of Health and Social Services (DHSS). Four authorities, called Health and Social Service Boards, act as agents for the Department. The Eastern Health and Social Services Board is centred around Belfast and is the largest, with a population of 647,600. The other three, the Western, Northern, and Southern Health and Social Services Boards, combined have a population of 941,800.

Since April 1991, each Board consists of six non-executive and up to six executive members and a non-executive chairman. The executive members must include the Area's General Manager and the Director of Finance. The non-executive members are drawn from the community at large and are selected by the Secretary of State for the individual contribution they make to the running of the board rather than representing any professional or local council groupings. Local business people are the commonest source of non-executive members.

The senior management team in each of the Northern Ireland boards consists of the executive members of the board along with other fellow officers who perform management roles. This is a change from the situation which previously prevailed when officers reflected strong professional interests. Area Health and Social Services Councils have been established as the body to represent consumer interests. Their members are in the main local councillors together with people from organisations with an interest in different care groupings. Whereas the Boards are supposed to listen to the voice of the consumer as expressed through these Area councils, the latter lack the teeth to ensure that cognizance is taken of their views.

For administration purposes, each Area is subdivided into Units of Management. Many units reflect the traditional dominance of hospitals at the expense of community care. The medical rather than the social model of care predominates.

During the early 1980s there were a number of key managerial initiatives affecting the NHS in Britain which had an influence in Northern Ireland as well. In general, there was a move towards greater accountability and better management. The UK Conservative Government commissioned an inquiry into the NHS management under the leadership of Roy Griffiths. The 'Griffiths' Report', as it became known, recommended that general managers should be appointed for every level of the NHS. Griffiths' terms of reference did not extend to Northern Ireland. Nevertheless, four general managers were appointed in 1985 in each of the four boards, but not until 1990 at the Unit of Management level (Carswell, 1985).

To understand the organisation of the Republic's system one needs to examine the 1970 Health Act. This was primarily designed to implement a reorganisation of general practitioner services and the regionalisation of hospital services. The latter objective resulted in the establishment of eight Health Boards. They are responsible for the provision of health services in their functional areas. Each health board is a body corporate, with the majority of members appointed by the local county councils and county borough corporations. The remainder of members must include persons elected by medical practitioners and members of other health professions. In contrast with Northern Ireland, the boundaries of the boards follow the boundaries of groups of counties. This facilitates inter-county arrangements for local government planning and development. The board areas try to avoid too many counties. Nevertheless, there are big discrepancies in the populations served by the boards. For example, the Eastern Health Board, which covers the counties of Wicklow, Kildare and Dublin (both city and county), serves a population almost six times that of the North Western Health Board.

In contrast to Northern Ireland, the Republic's health boards have had the equivalent of a general manager, known as the Chief Executive Officer, at the head of the board's management structure since 1970. He or she has three programme managers reporting to him or her covering the general hospitals, special hospitals (for the mentally ill and mentally handicapped) and the community care programmes. In addition to these four, functional managers for personnel, finance and management services go to make up the executive management team.

There is a major difference between the two jurisdictions in that the thirty voluntary hospitals and fourteen mental handicap agencies do not come under the control of the Republic's health boards. The hospitals are located in the major cities, especially in the east of the Republic, and provide most of the acute care in Dublin. The result has been that there are problems in controlling expenditure and in constructing an overall strategic plan for health.

Community care in the Republic means much more than a concept within social services. The community care services cover three broad areas:

(a) community protection services, including child health services, infectious diseases (immunisation and control), supervision of food and drink;
(b) community health; community nursing; community and infant care; dental, ophthalmic and aural services;
(c) welfare services, which include financial support by way of a range of income maintenance schemes; community support services such as home helps; and care of children.

The community care service accounts for about a quarter of the total annual budget. It is managed at the local or county level by Directors of Community Care. They have traditionally been doctors with no social work experience. It has led social workers to believe that as long as social work remains within a health model, it will never be treated with the seriousness it deserves.

Funding

Health is a labour-intensive industry and provides considerable employment throughout the island. In the Republic, approximately 58,500 people are directly employed in the public health care system, while 38,000 (full-time equivalents) are employed in Northern Ireland. This means that 24 persons per thousand are employed in health in Northern Ireland compared to 16 per thousand in the Republic.

Nurses constitute the largest proportion of health workers and make up about half of the total work-force. Despite the mix of public and private health care, the former accounts for the employment of the vast majority of health-care professionals. There are a significant number of self-employed contractors who work for the statutory system. General medical and dental practitioners and pharmacists for the most part fall into this category. There are around 1,800 general practitioners (GPs) and 1,200 dentists in the Republic, with the corresponding figures for the Northern jurisdiction being 930 and 480. In terms of the GP service, provision per 1,000 is roughly equal. There are 1,100 and 560 hospital consultants in the Republic and Northern Ireland respectively. Although this group are not the most numerous, much attention is paid to them because they traditionally commit a large proportion of expenditure while not always accepting the responsibility for managing the resources they control. One of the main focuses of debate has been devising a system whereby medical personnel can be brought into management while continuing to provide the high-quality professional service esteemed by the public in general. In Northern Ireland this has manifested itself in the Resource Management Initiative, which is being introduced into a number of large acute hospitals.

On the introduction of the Health Bill 1969, which sought to implement the re-organisation of health services, the Republic's Minister for Health stated:

the present government has not accepted the proposition that the state had a duty to provide unconditionally all medical, dental and other health service free of cost for everyone. Their policy has always been to design the services and the provisions on eligibility for them on the basis that a person should not be denied medical care because of lack of means, but that the services should not be free for all.

To appreciate the intricacies of the Republic's system and to understand the significance of this policy statement, one needs to look at the question of eligibility for health services. This question is not nearly so relevant in Northern Ireland, other than in a few areas such as dental fees and prescription charges.

Eligibility for free services was encoded in 1970 and then substantially amended by the Health Act 1991. Those under a certain income are 'eligible' for the full range of free health services and social care. Approximately one-third of the population and two-thirds of the over-65s now fall into this first category (Category I). Category II gives free or subsidised access to a range of services but excludes fees for GPs, pharmacists, dentists and opticians. Category II people are entitled to public hospital care, subject to a nominal one-off charge for out-patient visits and a similar charge per night for in-patient stays. There are some universal entitlements, for instance free drugs for certain long-term illnesses and maternity and infant care (Brady, 1992).

A large proportion of private funding comes through a state organised and subsidised health insurance company, the Voluntary Health Insurance Board (VHI). This Board was established in 1957 to provide cover for those not eligible for free hospital and specialist services – about 15 to 20 per cent of the population at the time. The main reason that people are now in the VHI is to have access to private hospital care and a consultant of their choice. Although the Board was introduced to enable the higher income group to obtain cover, the number who presently contribute and thus avail themselves of the benefits greatly exceed those outside Category I. The state encourages individuals to contribute to the fund by giving income tax relief on subscriptions at the marginal rate. Contributions to VHI are seen to be a good investment for those individuals who can afford them, especially as the marginal rate of taxation is relatively high. The attractions of the scheme include possible amenities such as accommodation in small wards, private rooms in the hospital of one's choice, choice of one's consultant and perhaps timing of operations.

The insurance scheme provides a means-tested system of entitlement to publicly provided services, supplemented by an overlapping state monopoly provision of insurance for private care (NESC,1990). Voluntary Health Insurance grew up so that the gap not covered by the limited eligibility would be eliminated. The services which insurance holders could use meant that more people saw that it was an advantage contributing even though they may have been classified as eligible for free health care. Such services include private wards and queue-jumping. In effect, the extra subscribers see this as a means of providing greater security and access. Contributions have been increasing for nearly all years since the inception of the insurance fund. Cut-backs in public health services have encouraged more people to become subscribers. When the individual's private payments are taken along with the insurance contributions, the total private spending amounts to 2.6 per cent of GDP. This rising figure is in contrast to a falling figure of 5.5 per cent for public health spending (Brady, 1992).

The financing of health services everywhere is a constant source of lively debate. The two main areas of debate are (a) whether the service is underfunded, and (b) the mix of public and private funding. The latter argument presupposes that there is a simple split between the two but in reality the situation is a lot more complex. Commentators suggest that the sources of money should be distinguished from the health care provider. While this distinction provides some clarification, the case of the Republic's health service system shows that in itself this is too simplistic. and would need to be supplemented by a mixture of the two categories. For instance, GPs are self-employed contractors and so their services are, in theory, privately produced. Their financing varies from one context to another. GP utilisation by the low-income group is publicly financed. Others who use the service are either privately financed or holders of insurance. It is argued that as this latter group of people contribute to the VHI scheme, which is tax-deductible, there is a mixture of private and public finance. Some services are unambiguously public in both their production and finance;

for example, the various vaccination programmes and school medical examinations receive services financed from general taxation and provided by the health boards.

One of the founding and dearly-held principles of the NHS (and associated Northern Ireland services) was that the services should be free at the point of consumption. As with the Republic, the bulk of expenditure is financed from central government. In Northern Ireland's case, it comes out of general taxation but also from individuals' contributions to national insurance. It means that services should be available to everyone irrespective of income. This means that the potentially most expensive service for the population, that of hospitals, is free. Other services, such as items on prescription and dentistry, are not free to everyone but in the main are subsidised by the state.

Monies for health and social services come out of the Northern Ireland vote, ie the funds for which the Northern Ireland Secretary is responsible. Perhaps because of this source, rather than coming from general NHS resources, a discrepancy has grown between the expenditure per head on health and social services in the rest of the UK compared with that in Northern Ireland. As much as 25 per cent is now commonly quoted as being the difference in favour of Northern Ireland.

The majority of health services in Northern Ireland have been supplied through the public sector. The private acute hospital sector is very small and accounts for very little of the total expenditure. The fastest growing part of private sector is in nursing and residential homes, particularly over the last ten years. Even here, the source of monies mostly comes from central government in the form of transfers from social security. As a percentage of total expenditure, very little comes from private spending whether from individuals or from private insurance.

In Northern Ireland's primary health care sector, general medical practitioners are independent contractors but are closely linked with the statutory sector in that they are paid from state funds on both a per capita and item-for-service basis. They have very few private, fee-paying patients. General dental practitioners charge their patients but also receive money from the state. Nurses in the primary sector are employed by the boards and so are paid from public funding.

Pressures for change Conclusion

Health is a major topic of political debate. It was a major issue in the 1992 general elections in both the UK and the Republic. There was much media comment on waiting lists for treatment by specialist medical practitioners, the opening of new hospitals and the closing of small local facilities. There is a natural tendency for critics to concentrate on institutional care, particularly when it involves large-scale public institutions. Obviously the hospital sector falls neatly into this picture, especially as it is a large resource-user. It is important to remember the part played in the community by the care provision outside hospital. Here the focus is on the care of people with chronic disability, for example, those who are physically disabled, chronically mentally ill, the mentally handicapped (now referred to as people with 'specific learning difficulties') and those with illnesses of old age. Care in the community may be provided 'informally' through families, friends, neighbours and volunteers or formally by the statutory social services, perhaps in partnership with voluntary organisations. There is a distinctive voluntary tradition throughout Ireland, much of which, especially in the Republic, is organised by religious orders.

The 1980s saw a world-wide interest in health-service delivery systems as many countries experienced concerns about rising costs, how to use resources more efficiently, providing greater choice, being more responsive to consumer preferences and about improving the quality of provision by releasing the potential for improved performance (Hunter, 1991). The methods through which these concerns are being addressed are, on the one hand, an examination of existing structures, roles and relationships and, on the other, an increasing interest in competition.

In the UK, there were misgivings after the 1987 general election, as the public perceived that the Government had 'cut' the NHS funds. A Government White Paper entitled 'Working For Patients' was issued in 1989 to address public concerns. There was something for every part of the health services. Some changes in administrative arrangements are already reflected in the outline given above. Others have come into effect during the last few years.

The major change affecting the whole of the UK brought about by the 'Working For Patients' document was the separation of the functions of purchasing and providing health services. In essence, this meant that the Area Health and Social Services Boards had a responsibility to divorce themselves from the direct management and involvement in the delivery of health and social services. They would concentrate on their purchase of health and social services. The Units of Management would be left to provide services to whoever wanted to purchase them. The opportunity now exists for boards to purchase services on behalf of their residents wherever they are going to get the best quality and value for money. This may mean purchasing services from other Areas, from authorities in Britain or boards in the Republic. From the Unit of Management's point of view, they could sell their services not only to their own but to other boards, authorities, or private health-care purchasers anywhere in Northern Ireland, Britain, the Republic or wherever. The internal market has arrived and contracting is the name of the game. Without contracts, there will be no income for the Units of Management. A 1990 White Paper dealing with Community Care ('People First') built upon the health reforms and emphasized a mixed economy approach of statutory, voluntary and private organisations participating in the market for social care.

The other reforms which are in the package allow for existing sections of the statutory sector to 'opt out' of the board system to achieve self-governing trust status. The idea is that Units of Management can be more independent of the board and have the freedom to organise more of their own affairs, for example, to set the wages of their own staff. Any profit which may be made will be ploughed back into the trust. The thinking behind this was to allow Units which were delivering services of high quality to be given the freedom to take initiatives and be rewarded for doing so. The other reform which could affect the working of the new market in health care is where General Medical Practitioners may be awarded funds to enable them to purchase services on behalf of their patients.

The reforms in the Republic have not yet gone down the road of internal markets, but the health services have not escaped considerable scrutiny in the last few years. New legislation to cover plans for the reorganisation of health services in the Eastern Health Board area is being drafted following the findings of the Commission on Health Funding, four reports from the Dublin Hospital Initiative Group, the Acute Hospital Efficiency Review and the Advisory Expert Committee on Local Government Reorganisation and Reform. The reforms have followed the line that there was a need to improve the administration of the health services. The failings identified include a lack of co-ordination between hospital and community-based services, the resultant over-involvement of the Department of Health in the management of individual services and the lost opportunities for achieving efficiencies through greater co-operation between different agencies. The reorganisation centres around the Eastern Health Board area. By establishing a single new authority responsible for all health and social services in the eastern area and responsible for determining broad service objectives and priorities for all services in the region, it is hoped that the Department of Health will be in a position to concentrate on strategic issues of objectives, financial allocation and evaluating service performance against general objectives. The new authority will administer services through five local areas, roughly the size of other boards. In addition, there is a need for greater clarity in relation to the roles, relationships and accountability of board members, their Chief Executive Officers, the Minister and Department, as well as to the other agencies involved in the delivery of the services. What underlies each set of reforms is a reaffirmation of the principle that the services should be there for the benefit of the patient or client. There is a problem in the Republic as a result of the insurance take-up, in that there is an accusation that the service is two-tiered. There is a similar fear developing as provider units in Northern Ireland decide on what they want to tender for. The issue of equity will emerge as both systems develop. Much has been written about the structure of the health systems. Structures, however, are only a means to an end.

Notes

1   Infant mortality rate per 1,000 live births

Highest other EC state	13.1 (Portugal, 1988)
The Republic of Ireland	8.2 (1990)
Northern Ireland	7.5 (1990)
Lowest other EC state	6.8 (Netherlands, 1988)

(Department of Health, Dublin)

References

Brady, M. (1992), 'Change and tradition', *The Health Service Journal*, 102, pp. 21–4.

Hunter, D. J. (ed.) (1991), *Paradoxes of competition for health*, Nuffield Institute for Health Service Studies.

NESC (1991) *A strategy for the nineties: economic stability and structural change*, National Economic and Social Council, Dublin.

9 *Reg North and John Coolahan*

Education

Since 1922 the education policies of the two new states on the island of Ireland have diverged radically on both administrative and curriculum issues. The Education Act 1923 in Northern Ireland, and subsequent legislation over the years, sought to give shape to education there in line with the general patterns and traditions operating in England and Wales. In the Irish Free State, and later the Republic of Ireland, no all-embracing education legislation was introduced. But, as part of the impulsion of political independence, different values and political forces shaped the educational system on very different lines from that of Northern Ireland. The systems grew steadily apart, and until recent years there was very little structured interaction or communication between them. So, from a contemporary perspective, they exhibit many contrasts and varying characteristics. This chapter attempts to capture the essential aspects of the two systems by outlining their structures and highlighting current trends and issues of concern.

The structure of educational administration

Central administration

There are fundamental differences in the way the two education systems are centrally administered. The highly complex structure of Northern Ireland's education administrative arrangements is the product of an interplay between a fifty-year legacy of English influence and accommodation of religious interest groups. In all essential respects it parallels the heavily structured arrangements found in England and Wales. The system is centrally administered by the Department of Education for Northern Ireland (DENI), which is responsible to an Education Minister appointed from the Northern Ireland Office. The Minister is either a member of the House of Commons or the House of Lords, served by a permanent civil service and a school inspectorate. Currently, under Direct Rule arrangements, there is no effective involvement by locally elected representatives in the development of educational policies. The sixty-strong inspectorate provides the professional evaluative linkages between actual school practices and a central policy formulation process that is also concerned with ensuring alignment with arrangements in England and Wales. There is a legal requirement for the inspectorate to offer professional advice on the formulation of education policy to meet the needs of pupils in Northern Ireland. The Education Minister, to whom it reports, is also responsible to the Cabinet in London and has strong interests in keeping the education system in line with English and Welsh legislation. There is clearly a basis for conflict of interests.

Compared with Northern Ireland, educational policy and control in the Republic of Ireland are highly centralised within the Department of Education, under a Minister responsible to the Oireachtas. There is no general advisory council for education, although specialist committees are convened on an occasional basis to report on particular issues. In 1987 a National Council for Curriculum and Assessment (NCCA) was established to advise the Minister on curricular and assessment matters. There is no intermediate body, such as regional educational authorities, between the Department and the individual schools, except the statutorily established Vocational Education Committees (VECs). Their main responsibility is for vocational schools, which cater for about 25 per cent of the second level pupils, but they also have responsibilities for aspects of adult education and for some third-level colleges. Moves in 1973 and in 1985 to establish regional educational authorities did not make progress. It is understood that the government has plans to make such a proposal again, giving limited powers to such agencies; the changing educational climate now may allow for a more receptive response. This may form part of a more wide-scale administrative restructuring, whereby the Department would hand many of its routine activities over to regional committees and individual schools and concentrate more on its strategic planning, accountability and budgetary roles.

Local administration

Differences in the degree of centralisation for the two systems are reflected in the arrangements made for local administration. Strategic administration at a local level in Northern Ireland is effected through five Education and Library Boards (ELBs). Their two main functions are the distribution of DENI-allocated financial resources to all maintained and controlled schools and the provision of advisory and support services to all schools. DENI directly funds the voluntary grammar school sector through a publicly stated formula. This central funding linkage also serves to emphasize the independence of voluntary grammar schools from local authority control. The Educational Reform Order (ERO), the current legislative provision, prescribes the roles and responsibilities of the ELBs, which parallel those of Local Education Authorities in England and Wales. It is in the membership of the boards that the main differences occur. Unlike England and Wales, where the membership directly reflects the results of local government elections, ELBs are not democratically accountable in the same sense.

The ELBs' membership is determined through appointment by the Education Minister. The general resulting pattern of membership is designed to reflect a range of interests: political parties from district councils; the transferrers (previous owners) of controlled schools; trustees of maintained schools; and those considered by the Minister to have interests in the services for which the board is responsible. In broad terms, this appointment system gives a Board composition ratio of 60:40 'non-political' to 'political' membership. The comparatively low political representation is, in part, justified by the particular funding arrangements for the education system. In this part of the United Kingdom, local rates do not make a contribution towards the support of education provision: it is directly funded by DENI out of the Northern Ireland Block grant.

Apart from Vocational Education Committees, there is no local government involvement in education in the Republic. Until recent years, most schools did not even have boards of management, and there are some secondary schools which still do not have them. However, it is likely that boards of management will be given more extended powers and responsibilities in the future. Parents, who enjoy very strong constitutional safeguards on their educational rights, have been taking a more directly active and centre-stage role on educational matters, particularly under the agency of the National Parents Council, established with state aid in 1985. Traditionally, the churches played a very significant role in school ownership, managership and school ethos at local level. A significant decline in religious vocations, coupled with considerable reflection on their priorities within Catholic religious congregations, have given rise to a retrenchment of religious involvement in schooling. This trend is likely to become more pronounced.

The school systems

There is a marked difference between the two school systems. In Northern Ireland seventy years of power struggles between state and non-secular interest groups have produced a school system divided by religious affiliation. In the post-primary sector, schools are also divided by ability through a centrally administered 'eleven-plus' selection test. Relatively easy access to prestigious grammar schools for most middle-class children, either through success with the 'eleven-plus' examination or by fee paying, has repressed any demands for independent secondary schooling. The resulting bi-partite system is equally divided into maintained (mainly Catholic) schools and controlled (mainly Protestant) schools, which in the post-primary sector are further sub-divided into grammar and secondary intermediate schools.

To retain some degree of autonomy for the management of its schools, the Catholic church, unlike the Protestant church, did not transfer its schools to the northern state in 1922. However, autonomy has its costs. Whereas the controlled sector receives 100 per cent funding, the maintained sector is required to provide 15 per cent of its capital costs. In practice, primarily because of the time-gap between initiation of capital expenditure and its reimbursement by DENI, the actual capital outlay by the Catholic church is nearer to 20 per cent. The effects of comparative under-funding of the maintained sector have yet to be assessed, although some of the reasons for the differences in educational attainment between Protestant and Catholic pupils outlined below might lie in this area. As a means of offering additional guarantees for their autonomy, recent legislation through the ERO established a Council for Catholic Maintained Schools (CCMS) to assume authority for the management, control and planning of Catholic maintained schools and act as the employing authority of teachers within the Catholic maintained sector. One effect of this novel arrangement is to diminish further the areas of responsibility of the ELBs, again bringing into question the need for rationalisation of local authority administration of the northern jurisdiction.

One of the most striking features of the Republic's education system is that, predominantly, it is a state-aided one, with the state providing most of the capital and current expenditure, although institutions are not generally publicly owned. Almost all schools are denominational, the great majority being Catholic, but no discrimination exists in the extent of the state funding between denominations. Recent years have seen the emergence of a small, but well-organised movement establishing multi-denominational schools under the 'Educate Together' banner. Education in primary schools and in over 90 per cent of second-level schools is free.

In 1991, 52 per cent of third-level education students in the Republic benefited from student grant schemes, some of which are linked to means tests and performance levels in the Leaving Certificate. In Northern Ireland all students accepted by a third-level institution anywhere in the United Kingdom or the Republic of Ireland will receive full payment of tuition fees from their Education and Library Board. These range from £1,800 per annum for an Arts degree to £4,700 per annum for a Medical or Dentistry degree. Interestingly, following a recent EC ruling, students from the Republic accepted by a third-level institution in the United Kingdom have their full tuition fees paid by the Government of the United Kingdom. This 'bargain' has been an influential factor in increasing the number of university students from the Republic coming into Northern Ireland. In 1990 approximately 10 per cent of the total undergraduate enrolment of the two northern universities came from the Republic. The financial consequences of this trend has not escaped the notice of some politicians.

Maintenance grants for Northern students at third-level institutions are means-tested. The proportion of Northern students receiving the full maintenance grant of £2,265 reflects the socio-economic balance between the west and the east of Northern Ireland. In the western half approximately 55 per cent of third-level students receive full maintenance support, compared with approximately 35 per cent in the north-east. On average, about 25 per cent of the students studying in third-level institutions do not receive any maintenance grant.

About 96 per cent of the Republic's children attend the national or state-aided primary schools, with only a small proportion opting for private primary schools in the main cities. Unlike Northern Ireland, where all pupils attend school from 5 to 16, schooling in the Republic is compulsory from 6 to 15, although about 85 per cent of the 4- and 5-year-olds attend national schools. It is planned to raise the minimum school-leaving age to 16 in the near future. There is no state support for other forms of nursery or pre-school education, whereas in Northern Ireland there are 85 fully state-supported nursery schools, located mainly in the socially deprived areas. The normal transfer date from primary to post-primary school is 12 years of age. In the Republic, unlike Northern Ireland, no formal test or examination exists at the end of primary school and no formal entry tests are sanctioned for entry into any form of post-primary school. Some schools hold entrance examinations themselves, sometimes justified on the basis of over-demand for places. An older, binary pattern of traditional, grammar-school-type education and vocational education has been eroded. Under state encouragement almost all post-primary schools (despite the existence of five official categories), offer a broadly comprehensive type of curriculum. The post-primary schools differ in the way they are funded and in aspects of ownership and, in some instances, in the type of pupils they enrol. There is, however, a great deal of homogeneity in the way schools operate and in their staffing, curricula, examinations and pedagogy. An older tradition of many single-sex schools has been changing rapidly with co-education now being accepted widely in all types of school.

Additional controls

Recent legislation has shifted the control of the vast majority of the curriculum content of the northern schools to DENI, acting through the Northern Ireland Curriculum Council (NICC). To facilitate the implementation of the legislated common curriculum, NICC combines the roles of the adviser to the Education Minister on curriculum matters and the publisher and distributor of approved curriculum materials. The Northern Ireland Schools Examination and Assessment Council (NISEAC) governs and conducts both public examinations (i.e. the General Certificate of Secondary Education (GCSE) and General Certificate of Education (Advanced level)) and assessment of the mandatory common curriculum. Whereas NISEAC has full discretion concerning the conduct of public examinations, although it must ensure that standards are recognised as equivalent to those elsewhere in the United Kingdom, assessment arrangements for the compulsory contributory subjects of the common curriculum must be carried out under conditions agreed by the Minister of Education.

In the Republic, the Department of Education exercises a preponderant role in determining educational policy, particularly with regard to curriculum, public examinations and inspectoral policy. Since 1987, the NCCA advises the Department on curricular and assessment matters and devises curricular programmes, subject to the approval of the Minister of Education. There are two public examinations: the Junior Certificate, taken after three years post-primary schooling, and the Leaving Certificate, taken at the end of post-primary schooling. The examinations are administered and controlled by the Department of Education. They rely heavily on terminal written examination papers. There is a desire in the Department to extend continuous assessment and school-based assessment by the teachers, but in current circumstances teachers have been resisting this. In direct contrast, the Northern Ireland government wishes to reduce school-based assessment in GCSEs and 'A' levels in the face of considerable opposition from a teaching profession happy with up to 50 per cent course-based work. Much of the time of the post-primary inspectorate has been taken up with the public examinations and a recent report on the future of the inspectorate called for significant change in their roles and administrative structures. The concept of a broad, comprehensive curriculum is promoted in the schools, right up to the Leaving Certificate, without the specialisation of the 'A' level type.

Patterns of educational provision

Participation trends

The last decade has seen a dramatic decline in the total number of pupils in both school systems. In the Northern education system this decline has not been uniform and, for the first time, there are more pupils in maintained schools than in controlled schools. This, however, understates the 'religious balance', given that there are many Catholics attending controlled schools and very few Protestant pupils attending maintained schools. There are now 14 per cent fewer pupils in primary schools compared with their peak of 214,300 in 1972. The greatest decline in pupil enrolments has been experienced by controlled primary schools. Indeed, since 1984, the maintained sector has seen a 5.9 per cent increase in pupil enrolments to 93,833. In the same period, pupil enrolments in controlled primary schools have decreased by 2.6 per cent, to 87,738. In the secondary sector this decline is still working its way throughout the system. Including grammar schools, the number of pupils attending secondary controlled schools has decreased by 16.7 per cent to 44,016. The greatest proportional decrease occurred in the Belfast area, where enrolments have fallen by a massive 29 per cent. During this period pupil enrolments in the maintained secondary sector have declined by approximately half that encountered in controlled schools: its pupil numbers fell by only 8.6 per cent to 45,952. Throughout this period voluntary grammar school pupil numbers have only decreased by 1 per cent, to 40,590. This relative protection from declining pupil numbers was in part due to an increased staying-on rate of students beyond 16. In part, too, grammar schools were cushioned by an increase of 2.5 per cent in pupils qualifying through the 'eleven-plus' examination to 37.1 per cent.

The Republic of Ireland has also experienced a very significant drop in its annual birthrate. Since 1980 the number of births decreased from 72,000 per annum to 51,000. This 29 per cent decrease in children entering education is already affecting enrolment in primary schools and will work its way through the system. While this development allows scope for improvements in the high pupil-teacher ratios which exist, nevertheless, there are direct implications for the future of small rural schools and for teacher employment. Pupil participation in post-primary schooling has expanded enormously over recent decades and the retention rates are impressive. Over 90 per cent of the 16-year-olds, 75 per cent of the 17-year-olds, and about 50 per cent of the 18-year-olds are in full-time education. Put another way, 73 per cent of the age cohort complete post-primary schooling. Of these, 80 per cent go on to participate in post-secondary education or training.

In Northern Ireland, numbers of pupils remaining at school beyond the statutory school-leaving age of 16 have also steadily increased during the 1980s. Compared with 1980, those aged 16 plus have increased from 36 per cent to 48 per cent, 17 plus from 25 per cent to 32 per cent, and 18 plus from 11 per cent to 14 per cent. Comparisons with the Republic of those in full-time education and training are, however, difficult to make because of the range of governmental training schemes that are in operation within Northern Ireland. There are clear trends of increased full-time participation in education and training at all levels.

Teacher resources

Although the last decade has seen a steady decline in the number of pupils – a decline that has been reflected in sustained teacher redundancies – teacher numbers in Northern Ireland secondary schools have decreased by only 6.2 per cent. This imbalance between pupil loss and teacher loss has resulted in an improvement in the secondary school Pupil-Teacher Ratio (PTR) from 15.4:1 in 1984 to 14.9:1 in 1989. In primary schools, however, teacher loss has broadly matched pupil loss, resulting in the PTR remaining static at about 23:1. When compared with England, Northern Ireland has a less favourable PTR, despite a legal requirement to deliver the same package of educational reforms. The overall PTR for England is 17.1:1, compared with 18.3:1 for Northern Ireland: a deficit of 6.5 per cent in teacher numbers. Pupil-teacher ratios in the Republic's schools have tended to be high. With reduction in pupil numbers it is expected that the PTR in post-primary schools is about 19:1. Thus, class sizes are higher in the Republic of Ireland than in Northern Ireland.

Teaching as a career traditionally has been held in high

social regard in the Republic, and it has continued to attract people of high intelligence and personal calibre. The changing demographic situation has led to reductions in the numbers permitted by the state to enter colleges of education. The closure of a major college of education in 1987 proved controversial and other forms of reorganisation and rationalisation between colleges and universities are now being undertaken. Teacher trainee numbers have also declined in university education departments, which train teachers for secondary teaching. The introduction of a six-year post-primary cycle, the increased retention rates, the expansion of post-Leaving Certificate Courses and improved PTRs may alleviate the worst aspects for post-primary teacher employment prospects in a declining pupil population. Those not obtaining full-time teaching posts at home are in big demand in English-speaking countries, and increased mobility, following mutual recognition of qualifications within the EC, opens other avenues of employment. More extensive in-service education for teachers is regarded as an issue of priority if planned reforms are to be achieved. In the Republic, a common salary scale exists for all teachers, with extra allowances for posts of responsibility and qualifications. The vast majority of teachers are members of the three unions which have proved strong and effective in defence of teacher interests. The largest union, the Irish National Teachers Organisation, has members in Northern Ireland as well as in the Republic.

Educational performance

The educational performance of students in Northern Ireland is frequently compared with their contemporaries in England and Wales. In particular, 'the retention of a selective system of secondary education has attracted attention, especially from critics of comprehensive systems'.[1] The general pattern of educational attainment, in terms of examination success, shows that students in Northern Ireland do significantly better than their English counterparts in GCE 'A' levels and GCSE examinations. However, the reverse is true at the other end of the ability scale, where the proportion of Northern Ireland students who leave the education system with little or no examination qualifications is twice that of students in England. Approximately 30 per cent of pupils leave school without attaining even one GCSE grade C. Thirteen per cent of school-leavers do not gain any qualifications at all.

Although comparisons with educational standards in England are illuminating, they are not the major focus of Northern Ireland. In recent years attention has been directed towards differences in educational attainment between Catholic and Protestant students. Osborne, for example, noted that 20 per cent of Protestant school-leavers gained two or more 'A' levels, compared with 16 per cent of Catholics.[2] In terms of subject balance, Protestant students enter and gain more passes in science subjects than Catholics, while the converse is the case in respect to arts and languages. In an attempt to explain differences in 'A' level attainment, Livingstone noted that 35 per cent of Protestants attended grammar schools compared with only 26 per cent of Catholics.[3] Livingstone's assertion is supported by school-leavers' qualifications from grammar schools in 1984 where there were no differences between Protestant and Catholic students' attainment, approximately half of whom attain two or more 'A' level passes.

Performance of students in the Republic in the public examinations is generally good, but, nevertheless, it is calculated that about 10 per cent or 12 per cent leave school without certification.[4] The transfer to varied forms of third-level education has increased greatly and now 38 per cent of the age cohort go on to such forms of education, the universities catering for 58 per cent of them. Overall, almost one-third of the whole population is engaged in full-time education. Sustaining this level of educational provision in a population with a high level of unemployment in the work-force causes financial strain. Expenditure on resources other than teachers and buildings is more limited than in other developed countries. At present, expenditure on education is about 6 per cent of GNP and amounts to 19 per cent of all public sector expenditure.

Current issues

This section addresses a number of education issues which appear to be of current concern within the two jurisdictions. The issues identified reflect the embedded conditions of the two systems. In Northern Ireland there are tensions generated from demands for legislated alignment with England and Wales and pressures for equity within. In the Republic, the issues tend to emerge from the exigencies for more rapid economic and social regeneration and accommodating changing demographic patterns.

Northern Ireland

The ERO has, in the main, created the agenda of current educational issues in Northern Ireland. It has introduced a new curriculum; created opportunities for increased parental choice and involvement through open enrolment; offered extensive delegation through the Local Management of Schools initiative and provided a framework within which Protestant and Catholic parents will find it easier to have their children educated together.

The ERO: the political context The major intentional theme running through the Education Reform Order is essentially one of choice.[5] The broad assumption is that through the exercise of choice significant players will engage market forces to bring about an improvement in educational standards. In essence, commodity has replaced service as a core concept. In place of mechanisms of bureaucratic planning and regulatory control, the disciplines of free-market exchange have been introduced to regulate the supply of the product.

When one compares the Reform Act for England and Wales with the Northern Ireland Reform Order there is almost a direct one-to-one correspondence. The most significant difference is in the omission of the mechanism that allows schools to 'opt out' of local authority control and achieve Grant Maintained Status. In the fairly predictable but unstable political climate of Northern Ireland, the possibility of schools 'opting out' of local control was thought to be too risky. The legislation did, however, provide for schools to achieve Grant Maintained Integrated Status.

The main effect of the Reform Order has been to shift power away from the bureaucratic middle ground of the Education and Library Boards to an entrepreneurial periphery, producing an education system where schools become the delivery points for the Government's reforms. Within this new political context, boards are required to make the transition from ultimate responsibility for the management of schools to the support of schools in their own management. The dual nature of the required change makes this transition more complex. Not only do boards need to build a support structure to assist schools with their new legal obligations, but they must also develop new structures and relationships that take account of the changed political context.[6]

The new curriculum   The establishment of a common curriculum entitlement for all pupils is likely to make an impact on the education system in a number of significant areas. Firstly, by requiring all schools to teach and assess a science and technology curriculum it may help redress the science/arts dichotomy between the Protestant and Catholic schools. Secondly, it will add the 'shove' to the long-standing 'push' towards more progressive primary schools.[7] Thirdly, by virtue of its commonality, it will assist in the long-term development towards a non-selective post-primary sector. Fourthly, the introduction of the topics 'Education for Mutual Understanding' and 'Cultural Heritage' might assist in lessening the divisions between the nationalist and unionist groupings. In the short term, however, the requirement for all pupils to study their cultural heritage will create conflict. As pointed out by Ievers, 'Some parents are fiercely pro-British and do not want their children to learn about Irish culture. Others are equally unequivocal in their insistence that their children only learn about their Irish heritage.'[8]

Although a common entitlement curriculum has its virtues, it also presents some undesirable outcomes. It will, for example, restrict a school's freedom of choice to offer their definition of a worthwhile experience to its pupils. In doing so, however, it 'challenges management to identify those emphases, additions and approaches in delivering the curriculum that will reflect a school's particular identity'.[9] In an attempt to facilitate schools in maintaining their own identity, the common curriculum has been designed around six areas of study, rather than the list of ten subjects of the national curriculum of England and Wales. It remains to be seen whether the acclaimed flexibility offered by this arrangement is 'real' or 'imagined'.[10] Secondly, the nature of the 'top-down' model has tended to further de-professionalise the teaching force by creating a belief in teachers that they are no longer masters of their own professional practice.

Local Management of Schools Local Management of Schools (LMS), paradoxically, provides the main political apparatus for central government control. It brings into sharp focus the labour-intensive nature of schooling. Schools are now discovering that about 75 per cent of their costs are directly related to teacher and ancillary staffing. Through delegating to schools individual budgets based largely on pupil numbers, schools are finding it necessary to shed staff in order to survive. Small schools, with their traditionally low teacher-pupil ratios, are the most threatened by the funding mechanisms of LMS. In Northern Ireland 61 per cent of its primary schools are classified as 'small schools'. The demographic effects of small rural school closure, particularly in western areas, may cause further shifts in the balance of Protestant and Catholic communities.

Funding of schools In an attempt to understand why there are higher levels of unemployment experienced by the Catholic community and lower levels of educational attainment, in comparison with the Protestant community, research was undertaken for the Standing Advisory Commission on Human Rights (SACHR). The subsequent report identified significant differences between the funding of Protestant and Catholic schools. With respect to recurrent costs, Catholic primary schools were found to be underfunded by 19.7 per cent when compared to Protestant primary schools. For secondary schools the difference was 11.0 per cent. Similar differences were identified for capital investment.

The reasons for this funding gap are complex and not fully understood. One possible explanation is that Catholic schools are trapped in a double bind. The formula used by the Education and Library Boards to allocate finance takes account of school building size and existing needs for resource maintenance. Catholic schools, when compared to Protestant schools, are relatively small, over-crowded and have low investment in technological and scientific resources, and therefore score low on the finance formula. They are in this condition precisely because they are under-funded. The requirement on the Catholic community to pay 15 per cent of capital charges also exacerbates the situation, particularly in the poorer parishes. There are other factors which have impact; for example, 'clawback' – the repayment of grant aid when a school is discontinued – affects the Catholic schools adversely when compared to Protestant schools. Also, Protestant schools are generally more favourably staffed with both teachers and ancillary workers. Steps to redress the imbalance are being examined by the Government and the Northern Irish bishops. It is possible that a reduction in the current capital expenditure requirement from 15 per cent to 5 per cent may satisfy the Catholic community.

Integrated schools   The ERO places a duty on the Department of Education 'to encourage and facilitate' the development of Grant Maintained Integrated Schools (GMIS). These are simply defined as schools where 'Protestant and Roman Catholic pupils are educated together'. Any school may achieve GMIS if more than 50 per cent of parents vote accordingly in a ballot requested by at least 20 per cent of parents. Inducements are offered in the form of priority investment considerations and full capital expenditure grants. To date only one secondary school and one primary school, both from the controlled sector, have applied for and achieved GMIS status. The Catholic Church remains critical of the GMIS legislation. They unsuccessfully challenged the legislation in the courts on the grounds that any attempt to remove a Catholic school from the control of its trustees without their consent would be illegal. The then Minister of Education, Brian Mawhinney, whilst noting the Catholic bishops' anxieties, offered his ideological commitment to parent forces to influence the education system by saying 'it is parents who will be influential in determining how the reform proposals will shape the delivery of education in Northern Ireland'.

As pointed out by Strain, 'there can be little doubt that government's commitment to the extension and strengthening of integrated education is ... firm and unqualified. But, paradoxically, the biggest hurdles facing these schools, and the policy they represent, lie in the public perceptions of what they stand for and of the possible political consequences'.[11] Less than 1 per cent of the school population attends non-GMIS integrated schools. These tend to represent small, predominately middle-class enclaves living outside those areas where sectarian strife is at its most virulent.

The Republic of Ireland

Education in the Irish Republic during the last decade came under the scrutiny of many specialist committees, the recommendations of which were not carried out in practice. A similar fate met many policy proposals set out in two government plans, the White Paper on Educational Development in 1980 and the Programme for Action in Education in 1984. Economic circumstances led to cut-backs in public expenditure with expanding services, such as education and health, being placed under particular financial constraint. Yet the momentum and expectation for educational reform were sustained and it would seem that by the mid-nineties the system will undergo significant change. The reports of the Primary Curriculum Review of Irish Education, the national council for curriculum and assessment reports, have contributed to a large agenda. Some of this agenda was taken up in the Programme for Economic and Social Progress agreed by the social partners in January 1991. As part of this Programme the government committed itself to the preparation of a comprehensive Green Paper on education, to be followed by a White Paper and a wide-ranging Education Act. The Green Paper was published in 1992. Among current issues of concern are curriculum, pedagogic and assessment reform; the planning of school provision for the declining pupil population; improved school management and a changing role for the school as an institution; inequality in educational provision and the education of minorities.

Curriculum and examination reform Since 1971 the primary schools have implemented a wide-ranging curriculum based on child-centred educational ideology. This is supported very much by the teaching force, although many constraints exist which inhibit the full implementation of the curriculum. No external tests or examinations are carried out. In line with thinking in Britain and elsewhere, policy makers are less supportive of the child-centred approach than formerly and seek more emphasis on the 'basics'. They also advocate the introduction of some external achievement tests. The practice in primary schools never became as 'progressive' as it is in English schools, and the drive for pupil testing is less intensive. In this, as in other features of education, the Republic's educational system has not experienced intense ideological conflict on policy.

Recent decades have witnessed much updating and restructuring of the post-primary curricula, accompanied by a good deal of curriculum development and experimentation. Yet the needs of a greatly expanded and changed pupil clientele and of wide-ranging social changes called for a more extensive reform programme for mainstream schooling. In 1989 the NCCA, with the approval of the Minister for Education, introduced radically new syllabuses for a new Junior Certificate Examination to be taken after three years post-primary schooling.[12] The programmes involve new curricular content, changed styles of pedagogy and more varied forms of assessment. Planning is also now well ahead for the introduction of a new curricular and assessment framework for senior-cycle education. All pupils will have the option of three years of post-primary education, leading to a new Leaving Certificate.

Many new social concerns are reflected in the changing curricular patterns, including closer liaison between the school and the workplace; greater emphasis on science and technology, modern languages and health education; more environmental awareness, and more comprehensive social and political studies. The changing curriculum is also intended to sustain a comprehensive policy: pupils of all ability levels and aptitudes can be accommodated in the same schools and take examinations in the subjects of their choice at appropriate grades of difficulty. A recent report of the Industrial Policy Review Group has called for a clearer demarcation between academic and vocational education. The new curricular, pedagogic and assessment plans pose significant problems for teachers. Teachers consider that there has been insufficient resourcing and in-service training to implement the new plans. Tension exists between the Department of Education and the teacher unions on these issues, and most specifically on school-based assessment for public examination certification purposes.

School planning and provision One of the key problems facing the Department of Education is the planning of school provision for a significantly declining pupil population. At post-primary level, the issue is also linked to a need to maintain a reasonable-sized school which can offer the planned range of curricular options to all pupils, particularly at senior level. This is difficult in a context where a quarter of such schools have less than 250 pupils and where a strong tradition of independence and isolationism exists between schools. Competition for pupil numbers may exacerbate such tendencies. The state is seeking to address the issue by fostering greater co-operation in the use of resources by small local schools, rationalisation and amalgamation of some schools and, where new schools are necessary, to establish large catchment schools with shared management arrangements. The decreasing involvement of religions will also contribute to a changed configuration of Irish post-primary schooling. Ten years hence it is likely that the Republic will have many fewer schools, but this will not be achieved without considerable difficulty, anxiety and redeployment of personnel.

Improved school management The Republic of Ireland is still affected by an old, deep-rooted tradition of school management by individuals or by nominated representatives of religious congregations. Management boards now exist for most schools and a partnership has been evolving between representatives of school trustees, parents, teachers and community interests. Increasingly, management boards are being urged to assume more responsibility and accountability for their schools. New budgetary arrangements are being devised on unit cost criteria. Managers will be encouraged to exercise more autonomy and discretion over school budgets, although payment of teacher salaries and large-scale building projects will remain under the Department of Education's control.

Management boards are being asked to prepare school plans, setting out for public reference policies on a wide range of school-related issues. They are also being urged to produce annual reports, which will make a great deal of relevant information available to parents and interested parties. However, the setting up of school league tables of results is not envisaged.

The roles of principals and senior staff are being redefined to create a more cohesive school management team. Demarcation of foundations and responsibilities will be more clearly established. The tradition of teacher individualism, very deeply rooted in the schools, may have to give way to a greater sense of teamwork and co-operative endeavour involving teachers and the wider school community. Schools are being encouraged to relate much more closely to their local communities in a variety of ways, so that they may be seen as a many-sided agency for promoting a higher quality of life in local communities. These changes involve significant attitudinal adjustments and the development of new skills which, in turn, are emphasizing the need for high quality in-service training in education management and administration.[13]

Inequality and treatment of minorities Equality of educational opportunity was a much-heralded political slogan in the sixties. Many reforms were introduced which expanded access to educational opportunity. Nevertheless, inequality of educational outcome persists with stubborn intensity, rooted in the socio-economic and domestic problems which impede educational progress for pupils. At the same time, educational achievement is the most predictive variable of occupational and economic attainment. The Green Paper laid particular stress on measures which make inroads into aspects of educational disadvantage.[14]

There has also been increasing concern about the protection and promotion of the educational rights of certain minorities. Recent years have seen commendable action of a specialised and scientific character on behalf of the 3 per cent of school children in various forms of special education. As in Northern Ireland, there have been moves to integrate handicapped pupils into mainstream schooling. This is only a gradual development, which must take account of parents' wishes and the availability of the appropriate resources in mainstream schools.

Compared with most EC countries, the Republic of Ireland does not encounter the same degree of problems in providing for multicultural education. Nevertheless, some problems do exist. The policy towards the education of the children of travelling people has moved towards greater integration of these pupils into mainstream schools. However, questions are being raised about the appropriate forms of curricula and teaching styles for such children. It is an area which seems likely to become a more prominent issue in the years ahead.

Groups of parents have been pressing for new forms of schooling that better match their preferences for their children. The move by parents to set up multi-denominational schools has been a striking instance. Within a generally more pluralist society, it would seem that this type of demand may develop further and lead to greater diversification of the schooling system. Significant questions are being raised about the constitutionality of rules for primary schools regarding religious provision, an issue which is addressed in the Green Paper on Education.

The demand for all-Irish language schools is another representation of a parent pressure group. The educational needs of the minority of native speakers of Irish, living mainly in the Gaeltacht regions, is also an issue of concern. The Irish language still holds a favoured position in educational policy, but its promotion and use have not kept pace with the expansion and general development of the education system. The EC has indicated concern for the survival of minority languages. With the drive toward greater use of other European languages for commercial, political and cultural purposes, the position of Irish is bound to become an issue of greater public debate in the years ahead. The overall impact of closer relationships with the rest of Europe on educational policy in the Republic will be a matter for interesting analysis in the future.

Conclusion

Taking an overview of education in the two parts of Ireland, some interesting parallels and varying emphases can be noted in contemporary patterns of educational development. On an administrative level, there are contrasting trends with moves towards greater centralisation of policy in Northern Ireland and a tendency towards devolution of responsibility and decentralisation in the Republic. The outcome may result in closer convergence in administrative balance of powers within both states. Each has been experiencing a significant decline in pupil numbers with consequent effects on the future of small schools, teacher employment and deployment and numbers in teacher education. For a variety of reasons, authorities on the two sides of the border have been encouraging greater pupil participation in post-compulsory schooling. High unemployment and the significance of educational certification for future employment prospects have emphasized the need to reduce drop-out levels and address very low achievement by some pupils. Both states have also been expanding training with the assistance of EC funding. This trend is likely to develop further in the post-1993 period.

Curricular reform has been a central issue of debate and policy throughout Ireland in recent years. There are many points of similarity in the new curricular emphases. Northern Ireland places more importance on testing and selection procedures, which lead to a highly differentiated pattern of post-primary schools. In the Republic of Ireland, there is little testing or selection and a more comprehensive post-primary curriculum exists. The public examinations for pupils in Northern Ireland are more firmly based on continuous assessment, where a greater degree of specialisation also occurs at senior levels.

The Republic contains a more homogenous community, less riven by religious and political conflict. Its school system is predominantly a state-aided, 'voluntary', denominational one. There is a decline in the involvement of religious personnel. The structure of schooling in Northern Ireland reflects greater community divisions. The moves towards integrated schooling and the introduction of 'Education for Mutual Understanding' and 'Cultural Heritage' initiatives reflect a concern to see the schools as agencies for fostering greater social cohesiveness. While not as striking, there are also moves in the Republic to foster greater cohesiveness through the Education Together movement, through reforms in the history and geography syllabuses and through greater awareness of the rights and needs of minorities. Both systems also seek to bring schools closer to their communities and wish to unleash a more pro-active, autonomous form of school management. There is greater emphasis on educational accountability and clients' rights in both jurisdictions. To date these may be merely seen as 'issues'. They reflect the gradual introduction of facilitating structures and arrangements, offering the potential of significant development at a future time.

Northern Ireland and the Republic of Ireland are two small states sharing a small island on the western periphery of Europe, a Europe that is undergoing historic and rapid change. Various initiatives, such as the school and pupil exchange schemes of Co-operation North, have helped to bring teachers and pupils together from each part of the island, yet gulfs of misunderstanding can exist between them. At an official level, a greater degree of liaison exists between the two administrations, fostered also by aspects of the Anglo-Irish Agreement. It remains to be seen how the distinguished and deep-rooted educational traditions of these two states may evolve, fructify and influence each other within the framework of the more integrated Europe of the nineties and beyond.

Notes

1 Cormack, R. J., A. M. Gallagher and R. D. Osborne (1991), *16th Report of the Standing Commission on Human Rights: Financing of Schools in Northern Ireland*, HMSO, London.

2 Cormack, J., A. M. Gallagher and R. D. Osborne (1987), 'Introduction' in R. D. Osborne, R. J. Cormack and R. L. Miller (eds.), *Education and Policy in Northern Ireland*, Policy Research Institute, Belfast.

3 Livingstone, J. (1987), 'Equality of opportunity in Northern Ireland' in R. D. Osborne, R. J. Cormack and R. L. Miller (eds.), *Education and Policy in Northern Ireland*, Policy Research Institute, Belfast.

4 Hannan, D. F., and S. Shortall (1991), *The Quality of their Education*, Economic and Social Research Institute, Dublin.

5 Department of Education for Northern Ireland (1989), *The Education Reform (Northern Ireland) Order 1989*, HMSO, Belfast.

6 Nolan, T. (1991), 'Implementing the Education (Northern Ireland)

Order: a personal perspective', *Management in Education*, V, 1, pp. 34–6.

7 Ievers, W. (1991), 'Critical management issues: a primary head's view', *Management in Education*, V, 1, pp. 37–8.

8 *Ibid*, p. 38.

9 Lord Belstead (1991), 'New framework for education in Northern Ireland', *Management in Education*, V, 1, pp. 31–2.

10 North, R. (1988), 'Restricted choice in the management of change', *Educational Management and Administration*, XVI, 3, pp. 163–72.

11 Strain, M. (1990), 'Opting out for integration', *Management in Education*, IV, 2, pp. 14–16.

12 McNamara, G., *et al*. (1990), *Achievement and Aspiration: Curricular Initiatives in Post-Primary Education in the 1980s*, Drumcondra Teachers' Centre, Dublin.

13 OECD (1991), *Review of National Policies for Education: Ireland*, Paris.

14 Breen, R. (1991), *Education and the Labour Market: Work and Unemployment Among Recent Cohorts of Irish School Leavers*, ESRI, Dublin.

Environment

The natural environment which forms the life-support system of our planet is gravely at risk. The earth's atmosphere is seriously threatened. The condition of water resources, including the sea, is causing concern, natural resources are being depleted and there is a growing loss of genetic diversity (European Council, *Dublin Declaration on the Environment*, 1990). Ireland, like its EC partners, has contributed to this environmental crisis and also has a role to play in finding a solution to this problem.

Environmental crisis at the global level

The depletion of stratospheric ozone is perhaps the most dramatic, as well as the most serious, example of global environmental degradation. The Republic, like other countries, has signed the 1985 *Vienna Convention for the Protection of the Ozone Layer*. This is a general agreement among nations of the world to work towards the protection of the ozone layer. As part of this agreement the Republic also signed the 1987 *Montreal Protocol on Substances that Deplete the Ozone Layer*.

Despite the 1987 Protocol, the extent of ozone thinning has increased. As a consequence, in May 1989 some countries agreed that they would aim for a total ban on the dangerous chlorofluorocarbons (CFCs) by the year 2000. The EC went further, however, and has prohibited the production of CFCs from the EC market by 1997.

The Republic has also been working with other EC member states to deal with the problem of global warming. In October 1990, for example, the Joint EC Council of Energy and Environmental Ministers agreed to stabilise Community emissions of carbon dioxide, one of the chief greenhouse gases. Furthermore, under the Helsinki Protocol, the Republic has agreed that it will reduce national sulphur dioxide (SO_2) emissions by 30 per cent by 1993. In May 1988, the Republic also signed the Sofia Protocol, which limits the emissions of nitrogen oxide (NO).

Acid rain is another worldwide environmental problem. Rainwater is naturally mildly acidic. Ireland is suffering from the problem of acid rain, although it is not as badly affected as other countries due to its peripheral situation on the western seaboard of Europe. Nevertheless, environmental groups, especially Earthwatch, have shown that the Moneypoint power station in County Clare is contributing to acid rain by causing a 50 per cent increase in Ireland's SO_2 emissions (Gormley, 1990).

Despite the various international efforts to deal with the environmental problems of ozone depletion, global warming and acid rain, many environmental groups have been highly critical of present international efforts to deal with our environmental crisis. Earthwatch, one of Ireland's main environmental groups, has argued that the reduction in emission levels agreed internationally for some of the most threatening substances is not adequate and that furthermore, the time scale given to governments to introduce these measures is too lax. The Air Pollution Act 1987, for example, gives the Minister for the Environment the power to prohibit the sale in the Republic of products that cause air pollution; critics say he could use these powers to ban the sale of ozone-depleting substances and thereby enhance the Republic's contribution to resolving the global environmental problem.

Environmental issues in Ireland

Many of Ireland's environmental problems have arisen as a consequence of the recent industrialisation and urbanisation of the country. Furthermore, under the influence of the Common Agricultural Policy (CAP), the island's traditional farming practices have been replaced by intensive agricultural production.

Industrialisation   Much of the Republic's industrialisation has been achieved by attracting foreign companies into the economy, where they establish branch factories (see Chapter 6 in this volume). These include foreign micro-electronic, pharmaceutical and chemical companies. The process of industrialisation brings with it numerous negative environmental effects. To begin with, individual plants can use large quantities of water in their production processes and frequently discharge industrial effluent into nearby watercourses. Both of these can have deleterious consequences for the quality of water in a region. The principal law in the Republic of Ireland regulating water pollution is the Local Government (Water Pollution) Act 1977. A recent amendment to this act, the Local Government (Water Pollution) (Amendment) Act 1990, increased the powers of local authorities with respect to water pollution control as well as increasing the penalties that they can impose on those found guilty of polluting.

Pollution in inland waterways is a serious problem in Ireland, although the problem lies as much in farming practices as it does with industry. Responsibility for control of inland waterway pollution in Northern Ireland rests with the Department of the Environment's Environmental Protection Division. Their activity is governed by the Water Act (Northern Ireland) 1972. They work closely with the Fisheries Division of the Department of Agriculture and its two Boards, the Fisheries Conservancy Board and the Foyle Fisheries Commission, to try and protect fishery habitats from pollution.

Many of the major environmental controversies in Ireland have arisen as a result of industrialisation. In particular, these controversies have been focused upon the pharmaceutical companies. Groups such as the Cork Environmental Alliance, an umbrella group co-ordinating the activity of numerous local environment groups in the Cork Harbour area, have been active in campaigns either to halt the establishment of particular factories or else to restrict the activities of those already in operation. Two of the most significant campaigns have been those seeking to halt the establishment of the Merrel Dow Chemical Company in East Cork and the Swiss company Sandoz in Cork Harbour because of the fear of pollution. Campaigns have also been conducted by individuals, the most important of which was that by the Hanrahan family in Clonmel, who fought a successful campaign against a multinational company, Merch Sharp and Dohme, which they claimed was responsible for the death of their cattle and the contamination of their farm land.

The lack of sensitivity of the Industrial Development Authority (IDA), the body with chief responsibility for Irish industrialisation, to the environmental record of multinational companies has led the environmental movement to argue that the IDA attracts 'dirty' industries into Ireland. This claim is denied by the IDA. Furthermore, the movement argues that Ireland, by having weak and ill-enforced environmental protection legislation, has acted as a haven for toxic industry. If these companies were to locate elsewhere they would incur heavy costs in installing pollution abatement technology.

Dealing with the waste generated by industry has been a recurring problem of Irish industrialisation. According to the European Commission, over 52,000 tonnes of toxic and dangerous waste are produced in the Republic of Ireland each year, as well as 75,000 tonnes of what it terms 'problematic waste', which includes chemical waste. The treatment of toxic trade waste, in particular, has been the chief source of environmental concern.

Since the early 1970s, various governments in the Republic

have sought to deal with this problem through the establishment
of a national toxic dump and incinerator. However, numerous
sites identified as possible locations for such a toxic dump
have seen the growth of local opposition, which has effectively
forced the government to abandon its plans, time and time
again. Using co-operation procedures established under the
Anglo-Irish Agreement, the Republic's government sought to
locate the national waste incinerator in Northern Ireland. As
a consequence, Du Pont, a chemical company, investigated
the possibility of establishing this incinerator at its Maydown
plant located outside Derry city. However, over sixty local
environmental and community groups opposed this plan. In
December 1991 Du Pont abandoned this plan and Ireland's
disposal of its toxic waste continues to be a major environmental
concern.

In addition to the waste produced by industry, there is also
other solid waste arising from domestic, commercial, mining,
quarrying, construction and agricultural sources. Both Northern
Ireland and the Republic produce a very large amount of this
type of waste each year. Traditionally, most of it has been
dumped in landfills and overall there has been no coherent
policy on the management of this waste.

The traditional method of disposal of waste in landfills causes
numerous environmental problems. To begin with, it can cause
the build-up of methane, a greenhouse gas. Furthermore, as
the volume of waste in recent years has dramatically increased
due to the rise of packaging and disposable products, many
landfill sites have become full. It is difficult to obtain local
government approval for new sites, particularly as conservation
groups campaign against the encroachment by refuse dumps
on wildlife habitat, especially on the marine foreshore. Due
to these environmental pressures, as well as concern about
economic misuse of the earth's finite resources, the European
Commission became actively involved in the regulation of waste
disposal.

The European Commission has issued a number of directives
on the disposal and treatment of waste. These directives

have made it compulsory for all county councils to establish an integrated waste management programme, aimed at the recycling, collection, recovery and treatment of domestic waste, industrial waste and sewage. As a consequence, the Republic's county councils have had to fund projects aimed at a more ecologically balanced approach to dealing with waste. For example, a new Tallaght-based co-operative is currently experimenting with kerb-side recovery of domestic waste and the recycling of waste. A similar programme, known as 'Northern Ireland 2000', has been set up in Northern Ireland. Its aim is to encourage recycling by creating partnership between industry, local authorities and voluntary groups. Waste, it is argued, is a valuable resource and without recycling, materials such as glass, plastic and metals will be unnecessarily discarded. Furthermore, it is argued, recycling can create employment.

The area of recycling has seen considerable involvement by environmental groups. Earthwatch, for example, runs a school-based recycling campaign, encouraging pupils to become involved in the collection of domestic waste, including glass, paper, plastic and tin, for recycling. However, infrastructural problems exist and the country as a whole lacks proper collection facilities and has insufficient factories to handle the amount of material available for recycling. Northern Ireland currently has no glass recycling factory, nor has the region the capacity to recycle the volume of paper that is being collected. As a consequence, environmental groups have been calling for greater commitment to recycling in both Northern Ireland and the Republic.

It used to be thought that Ireland was devoid of mineral wealth. However, as recent geological surveys in both Northern Ireland and the Republic have revealed, Ireland has very rich deposits of key minerals and metals. Gold, uranium, silver, lead, zinc, gypsum and lignite are just a few of the deposits that have recently been found, sometimes in large, commercially-viable quantities.

Mining in Northern Ireland is regulated by the Mineral Development Act (Northern Ireland) 1969, and the Minister for

Economic Development has overall responsibility for the area
of mineral exploration and development. A company wishing to
engage in mining first applies to the Minister for a prospecting
licence and if prospecting shows that commercially valuable
mineral deposits exist, then a full mining licence is sought.
By 1991, twenty-six mineral prospecting licences had been
granted in Northern Ireland to mining companies, as well as
three licences to search for petroleum. These companies are
awaiting the final results of prospecting to see if full mining
licences are worthwhile.

In the Republic, the Department of Energy has responsibility
for mineral exploration and mining, as well as the exploitation
of natural gas and petroleum. The Minerals Division of the
Department is responsible for mineral exploitation and, similarly,
the Department's Petroleum Affairs Division has responsibility
for the petroleum deposits. The Department also has a Mining
Board and chief among its responsibilities is the settling of
compensation claims arising as a result of mining, in particular,
damages to land that are a result of mineral exploration.

The extraction industry is the source of one of the main
pressures currently being exercised on the Irish government.
Environmentalists argue that mining causes severe environmental disruption. Gold mining, for example, requires the use
of cyanide, which pollutes water tables, river courses and the
land. Similarly, the tailing ponds from uranium mines remain
radioactive for centuries. Furthermore, after mineral extraction
the land is often of little use for other, more traditional forms
of activity. This is important, as many of the mineral deposits
identified in the Republic are in scenic locations which rely
heavily on tourism and fishing. These activities are often severely
disrupted by mining. The prospect of gold mining in Doolough
in County Mayo, in an area of outstanding natural beauty and
one of Europe's last unspoilt regions, is one such example.

For many local communities, mining poses a very stark
choice: the attainment of short-term economic gain at the
expense of long-term sustainable economic development. The
Lignite Action Group, for example, a group opposed to lignite

mining in Lough Neagh, saw mining in these terms. For the group, lignite mining meant the swapping of prosperous eel fishing and leisure activities at the local level for economic profits for multinational companies. Furthermore, Lough Neagh is an international bird sanctuary and is protected by the Ramsar Convention on the protection of wetlands, to which the UK is a signatory. This, argued Lignite Action, should be enough to prohibit mining in the lough area.

Mining has been beset by environmental controversy in Ireland. Neither the Republic nor Northern Ireland governmental policy, argue environmentalists, has taken the interests of local economic activity or the environment seriously. For this reason, environmental groups have mushroomed in areas where prospecting and mining licences have been issued. In 1990, recognizing that mining is a national and not just a local issue, many of the leading groups united to form an umbrella group called Minewatch, to share information and to provide mutual support for campaigns.

Groups are also beginning to examine the issues of quarrying and peat extraction. Excessive peat extraction is causing many environmental problems in Ireland. The Irish Peat Land Conservation Council has expressed concern, especially over the increased use of mechanical turfers, and they fear that, unless protected, all raised bogs in Ireland will be destroyed by 1997. Many of Ireland's blanket and raised bogs are of international importance and Ireland is one of the few countries left in Europe where a wide range of peatland still exists in a near-natural state. A blanket bog consists of a carpet of peat spread over a large area of land. A raised bog is dome-shaped, having developed in a former lake basin in the midland counties. Bogs are important flora and wildlife habitats and support a number of rare plants and animals, including bog orchids and slender cotton grass, as well as the Greenland white-fronted goose. The European Parliament has recognised the importance of preserving Irish bogs.

The Republic's government has recently responded to both national and international pressure to preserve Irish bogs.

Under its Environmental Action Programme of 1990, the first comprehensive environmental programme ever adopted by an Irish government, it has acquired for conservation purposes a number of hectares of blanket and raised bog in counties Mayo, Galway and Offaly, as well as in Roscommon. However, despite these gestures many bogs have been irreparably damaged and only a small fraction of internationally important raised and blanket bogs are currently protected.

Agricultural modernisation   Under the influence of the CAP, Irish farming has undergone radical change. From the dominance of mixed farming techniques and the presence of labour-intensive farming practices, Irish agriculture has changed to being highly capital-intensive. Most noticeable is the change to intensive cattle production. This has resulted in a flight of people from the land, an increase in the size of holdings as well as what may be termed the development of agribusiness in the place of farming. The changing nature of Irish agriculture has resulted in new and very intensive environmental pressures and agriculture has become one of the chief causes of pollution in contemporary Ireland.

There are a number of characteristic modern farming methods of particular significance from an environmental point of view. Many problems arise from the methods of intensive production. These include the practice of 'zero grazing', that is, the rearing of farm animals indoors, such as chickens, cows and pigs. Such conditions often are prime locations for the development of diseases, which in turn require the constant use of drugs such as antibiotics on the animals. Environmental groups in Ireland have expressed concerns at the residue of drugs found in farm products, especially milk and meat, as a result of this practice. Intensive production can also include using artificial feeds and light in order to increase yields beyond what would be obtained in more 'natural' settings, forcing farmers to resort to non-natural feeding practices, such as feeding cows, naturally vegetarian animals, the carcasses of other animals. This has resulted in the spread of a new and dangerous disease, Bovine Spongiform Encephalopathy (BSE), the so-called 'mad cow disease'. Recent revelations of its spread to domestic cats and among zoo animals have heightened fears of transmission of this disease to humans.

Furthermore, intensive production has resulted in the build-up of farm effluent, which has tended to be dumped in inland waterways. This has resulted in major and repeated fish kills along Irish rivers and lakes. One of the symbols of bad agricultural practice in Ireland can be found in the history of the extensive pollution of Lough Sheelin, a lough system that became heavily polluted as a result of slurry spreading by local farmers. The Republic's Environmental Action Programme has devoted £50,000 to help deal with this problem. Further problems have arisen as a result of the excessive use of fertilizers, pesticides and fungicides. This results in the phenomenon known as 'eutrophication', that is, the growth of an algae-bloom on waterways, starving existing life systems of vital oxygen. The Rivers Blackwater, Suir and Shannon are affected by this problem.

Intensive farming also presents other environmental problems, including drainage of wetlands, which are important wildlife and flora habitats, and excessive hedge cutting. One such drainage scheme on the Blackwater was carried out by both the Northern Ireland and the Republic's governments using EC funding and it has come under repeated criticism from conservation groups, angling and fisheries organisations, as well as some farmers in the area. Wider criticisms have also been made. The RSPB, for example, has been very critical of modern farming practices introduced under the CAP, and has called for their radical reform.

Dealing with the environmental problems of modern agricultural practice requires more than the allocation of blame to individual farmers, however. The problem has its roots in the CAP as well as the so-called 'green revolution', that is, bumper harvests from a diminishing variety of crop strains requiring ever-increasing amounts of fertilizers, pesticides and fungicides to produce from an exhausted soil. It is to this problem that many in the organic agriculture movement have turned their attention, and bodies such as the Irish Organic Food Growers' Association (IOFGA) have encouraged a radically different and sustainable farming practice. Much of the philosophy of IOFGA, which is expressed in their magazine *Common Ground*, is based on the use of the land in a renewable manner as well as the utilisation of products, techniques and skills that are appropriate to the local climate and soil conditions. As interest in the commercial viability of organic agricultures spread, the Republic's government in its 1990 Environmental Action Programme devoted £450,000 to the development of Irish organic farming.

Despite the serious pollution and environmental problems that arise as a result of farming practices, the Irish environmental movement as a whole has not been very forthcoming in its critique of Irish agriculture. The main critique of farming has come from the older, traditional conservation movement. Bodies such as the Ulster Wildlife Trust, for example, have been among the most vocal.

Forestry is a difficult and somewhat paradoxical area for environmentalists. The planting of trees is considered of prime importance among conservationists as it helps stop soil erosion and provides habitat for wildlife, while short-rotation forestry can help Ireland reduce its use of non-renewable resources in the production of energy. Furthermore, forest planting can reduce the high levels of wood from tropical rain forests that are currently being imported into Ireland. Forestry can also make a contribution to both employment and the balance of trade. Its development in Ireland is supported by EC funds. While acknowledging these benefits, however, conservationists have expressed concern at the nature of modern forestry.

In particular they are concerned with the lack of diversity in species of trees planted, with heavy reliance on conifers, in particular Sitka spruce. In 1988-89, 74 per cent of trees planted in Northern Ireland's forests were Sitka spruce. While conifer plantations appear to be more economically profitable in the short term, they contribute to soil acidification and do not create a rich and varied habitat for flora and fauna. In contrast, broadleaved woodlands provide a richer habitat for wildlife and have a more varied and natural appearance than the blanket effect of conifer plantations. In addition, conifer plantations are often situated on upland bogs, which are rare in international terms and important sites for flora and fauna. Recognizing these problems, Crann: The Irish Woodland Trust, which was founded in 1986, is working towards the re-treeing of Ireland with broadleaved trees. In an effort to address these environmental concerns, all major re-forestation programmes in the Republic now require an Environmental Impact Assessment.

As a consequence of decades of over-fishing, commercial fishing is now in crisis. Smaller catches have led many fisherm to have recourse to landing immature fish, thus deepening the problem. Fishing is now regulated by the EC and, as part of its common fisheries policy, the EC has imposed fish quotas upon its member states. The recent development of commercial fish farming has also added to the pressures that fishing places upon the environment.

In the late 1980s, fish farming developed rapidly in Ireland, especially in the Connemara region. However, the commercial advantages of fish farming soon became overshadowed by environmental concerns. Among these concerns was the fear that fish farming could endanger wild fish stocks and pollute fish habitat. For example, wild salmon stocks could be altered genetically through interbreeding with escaped farm fish. Similarly, waste material, food and chemicals used for treating disease in farmed fish could also pollute the bay or harbour in which the fish cages are located. Earthwatch has published a report on fish farming, in which they point out the dangers to other marine life of fish farming, including dangers from the discharges into the sea of the chemical 'Nuvam', used to treat the sea lice that develop on farmed fish (Earthwatch, 1989).

Following these expressions of concern, the Republic's Department of the Marine, which has responsibility for fish farming, set up an Advisory Body to look into the environmental problems associated with fish farming. As a result the Minister

for the Marine intends to bring the fish farming industry
under full licensing and monitoring by the end of 1991. It is
expected that the new Environmental Protection Agency will
take responsibility for this licensing.

In Northern Ireland the law requires all fish farms to be
licensed by the Department of the Environment as well as the
Department of Agriculture. A third licence is also required
from the Crown Estate Commission. However, at present there
is only one salmon farm in Northern Ireland but there are
twenty-one commercial trout farms currently under licence.

Commercial fisheries themselves also suffer from the consequences of other forms of human activity and in particular,
inland waterway and marine pollution. This pollution can be
traced to sewage disposal, a noticeable problem in areas of
high population density, discharge of industrial waste and
environmentally insensitive disposal of farm effluent.

The problem of waterway and marine pollution is most
noticeable along the east coast and the Irish Sea. The 'Coast
Watch Survey' carried out by the Dublin Bay Environmental
Group found that the eastern coastline was contaminated by
raw sewage pollution. As part of its campaign to clean up the
Irish Sea, Greenpeace has launched 'a clean seas campaign' and
is actively working with environmental groups along the eastern
coast, as well as in Wales and England, to ensure that both the
Irish and British governments are forced to implement policies
to clean up the Irish Sea.

One of the most serious causes of pollution of the Irish
Sea is the discharge of radioactive waste from the British
nuclear reprocessing plant at Sellafield. This can also have a
deleterious effect on fisheries. As a result of these discharges,
environmental groups claim that the Irish Sea is the most
radioactive sea in the world. Reports by monitoring agencies
confirm this problem. The plant's poor environmental record,
as well as its close proximity to the major centres of population
on the Irish east coast, have led all the main political parties in
the Republic, at the local as well as the national level, to call for
the closure of Sellafield.

Urbanisation Urbanisation, especially if it brings with it poorly planned suburban housing sprawl, can also pose severe threats to the environment. The Dublin area, for example, grew by 42 per cent between 1966 and 1986. This growth, by encroaching upon the surrounding countryside, placed severe pressure on wildlife habitat. Concern over a similar problem in Belfast led to the formation of the Belfast Urban Wildlife Group. Their aim is to protect urban wildlife in the face of new urban development plans.

Ribbon housing development is also a problem. According to the report on the state of the Republic of Ireland's environment published by An Foras Forbartha (the former national institute for physical planning and construction research), the output of 'one-off' houses in rural areas increased from 5,530 to 11,050 between 1976 and 1983 and they now account for over half the houses built in the country. Most of those living in rural housing are not engaged in agriculture and commute to their place of work in the nearest town or city. Ribbon housing development leads to the spread of urban blight, loss of agricultural land as well as a blurring of the distinction between the countryside and the city. This problem is not confined to the east coast: An Foras Forbartha (1985) found a noticeable pattern of ribbon development between Galway city and Connemara. Many of the houses are modern bungalows that do not fit well into the local landscape. Ribbon development combined with poor housing style can threaten not just the countryside but also the quality of the visual landscape.

An Taisce, one of Ireland's leading environmental groups, with a membership of over 6,000, has been actively involved in the protection of Ireland's environmental heritage. This includes protecting the island's unspoiled environment by encouraging the continued use of old buildings of quality, as well as the preservation of traditional cottages and ancient burial sites. They have also been active in the opposition to the destruction of old Georgian Dublin, especially in the face of new office and car park developments. Furthermore, they have campaigned for the preservation of the quality of the visual landscape by urging the introduction of a more fitting style of housing, which uses native materials as well as design.

High concentrations of population bring sewage disposal problems. Both the discharge of sewage to inland and marine waterways as well as the standards of drinking water is now governed by laws, many of them originating from the EC. The European Commission Directive on Urban Waste Water Treatment, for example, came into effect in the Republic in May 1991. This law fixes standards for sewage treatment and also requires governments to stop sewage sludge disposal by 1998. As a consequence of this EC policy, the Republic's government is now committed to the phasing out of raw sewage discharges.

Environmentally insensitive disposal of sewage has led to pollution problems, especially in relation to the quality of bathing water. The EC has a system of monitoring the quality of water at beaches and in 1990 it issued 48 'Blue Flags' – that is symbols of quality – to Irish beaches. The Republic's Department of the Environment is committed to increasing this number by aiding local authorities in upgrading the quality of water at Irish beaches.

Urban sprawl increases the use of cars for commuting, thus adding to city air pollution as well as the greenhouse effect. This problem is exacerbated by inadequate public transport, for which Dublin is notorious. Air pollution is a major problem facing modern cities and Dublin is no exception. In the late 1980s, the levels of smog – a word meaning both smoke and fog – in Dublin developed into a major political issue. In the seven years prior to 1990/1 national or EC air quality standards for smog were breached on average in Dublin eleven times each winter. The main source of this smog was the burning of bituminous coal from domestic fires. More than 60 per cent of Dublin householders burn coal as their main form of heating. The World Health Organisation (WHO) has said that high levels of smog can lead to an increase in mortality rates, as well as in the number of people admitted to hospitals.

Following public outcry, the Minister for the Environment began trials in Ballyfermot of home heating using smokeless fuel.

Then in 1990 the Minister introduced a regulation under the already existing Air Pollution Act 1987 banning the marketing, sale and distribution of bituminous coal in Dublin. The local authorities are responsible for enforcing this ban.

Further measures have also been taken by the Republic's government in an effort to improve air quality. The Air Pollution Act 1987, for example, gives the Minister for the Environment and the local authorities powers to deal with air pollution from industry which poses a danger to health, to flora or fauna, which may damage property or interfere with the amenities of the environment. The government has also reduced the tax on unleaded petrol, making it cheaper than leaded petrol. By 1991, sales of unleaded petrol amounted to 23 per cent of total petrol sales. However, Ireland still lags behind its European neighbours and has a long way to go to match Germany, where unleaded petrol sales amount to nearly 70 per cent of all petrol sales.

Many people, especially those who live in urban settings, see the countryside as providing a retreat from the pressures of life and as a pleasant environment in which to spend their leisure time. While access is important, this use can place severe strains upon the countryside, particularly on local flora and fauna. Littering and trampling upon vegetation can threaten habitats and noise can disrupt wildlife, especially nesting birds. Such problems have led to the establishment of organisations such as the Association of Lough Neagh Users, which tries to reconcile the differing pressures put upon the lough by recreational use, such as water skiing and boating; fishing, both for leisure and commercially; and conservation needs as well as economic activity. A similar body exists for Strangford Lough.

The use of the countryside and the protection of flora and fauna is governed by international and national laws. Northern Ireland has one site, Lough Neagh and Lough Beg, protected by the Ramsar Convention. The Republic has many more, with fifteen Ramsar sites, nine of which are peatlands. However, environmentalists in Northern Ireland have been critical of the UK government for failing to designate sufficient sites under the Ramsar Convention. The Royal Society for the Protection of Birds (RSPB) has identified very important sites for wildfowl that should be given protection under this Convention. Other laws in Northern Ireland and the Republic have arisen out of legislation that has been formulated at the EC level. The European Commission Directive on the Conservation of Wild Birds, introduced by the EC in 1977, for example, is a key law governing wildlife and habitat conservation.

The main law governing the protection of wildlife in the Republic is the Wildlife Act 1976. This law protects wild flora and fauna and also provides for conservation of areas having specific wildlife value. In the Republic the government designates important sites as Nature Reserves or National Parks. Despite this law, however, wildlife remains under threat. Changing farming practices are one source of danger. The once abundant corncrake, for example, is now an endangered bird in Ireland. Until recently, Irish meadows offered the corncrake one of its last European sanctuaries, but the modern change from hay-making to silage has proved disastrous to the bird's habitat. Similarly, hedge-cutting during the nesting season is illegal. Farm drainage and the excessive use of pesticides and fungicides is also causing the loss of habitat and wild flowers. The Irish Wildbird Conservancy have expressed concern about the loss of habitats for birds.

Conservation is a key issue for environmentalists in Northern Ireland. There are a number of important voluntary organisations that are very active in the area of conservation; chief among these are the National Trust, somewhat equivalent to An Taisce, the RSPB, the World Wildlife Fund for Nature, the Ulster Wildlife Trust, as well as the Conservation Volunteers. An umbrella organisation, the Northern Ireland Environment Link, was recently established to help a number of the North's key environmental groups to exchange information more easily and lend each other mutual support in campaigning.

By now it will be clear that the Irish environment is currently subject to many pressures. The context within which these pressures are occurring, as well as the policy responses of the governments of Northern Ireland and the Republic, have been outlined. It is clear that these policy responses have not occurred in a vacuum and that international bodies, in particular the EC, have played a central role in framing them. Irish environmental groups have also been influential in shaping these policies and the positions adopted by many of the leading Irish environmental groups have therefore been examined. Some indication has been given of the regulatory framework within which environmental issues are being considered. However, in order to complete this picture, a clearer exposition of the laws, as well as the administrative framework within which policy is formulated and implemented, is needed.

Administrative structures and the laws

Both the laws and the administrative structures relating to environmental issues have undergone profound changes during the last few years. Part of the reason for this lies with the EC's increased involvement in environmental matters. The EC's approach to the environment has relied heavily upon the use of the law, in particular Directives. This in turn has required the governments of Northern Ireland and the Republic to introduce a host of new legislation dealing with such matters as air quality, water quality and waste disposal, as well as protection of wildlife. Furthermore, as the volume of work increases and the areas requiring environmental control continue to expand, changes have occurred in the agencies and administrative bodies responsible for environmental protection.

The Republic of Ireland The Department of the Environment, under its Minister, has overall responsibility for the protection of the environment. The Department guides and co-ordinates at the state level the activities of local authorities in environmental matters. The Department also administers the 'Environment Works (Youth Employment) Scheme' as well as annual 'Environmental Awareness Week'. The Minister for the Environment has overall responsibility for the Department and the Minister of State has responsibility for matters directly relating to pollution control and environmental protection. Currently, the Department's main priorities are in the areas of pollution control and planning development control.

Other government departments have responsibility for environmental matters; for example, the Department of Energy is responsible for petroleum and mineral development, including the issuing of mining licences, and for pollution control during petroleum exploration. The Nuclear Energy Board also reports to this Department. The Department of Agriculture and Food is concerned with pollution as it affects agriculture, as well as the pollution arising from modern agricultural practices. The Department of the Marine licenses discharges of pollutants at sea, and is also concerned with the conservation of marine wildlife and the regulation of fish farming. The Department of Labour also has a role to play, for example, in its responsibility for the protection of workers exposed to pollution. Furthermore, the Department of the Taoiseach has responsibility for the National Heritage Council.

As can be seen from the above list, the control of pollution and the protection of the natural environment is a complex business. Responsibility is spread over a large number of government departments and governed by a variety of different laws. As a consequence, the approach to environmental protection in the Republic often lacks consistency and coherence.

Some responsibility for environmental matters rests with regional and local authorities. Regional development organisations, such as the County Committees of Agriculture, the Fisheries Boards and the Harbour Authorities, all have specific environmental responsibilities that arise directly from their main areas of competence. However, local authorities are in many respects more important and they play a key role in monitoring the environment and ensuring that the state's environmental laws are properly implemented. They are also responsible for two very important functions: planning and sanitary provision.

Planning in Ireland is covered by a variety of Local Government (Planning and Development) Acts dating from 1963. Any person who intends to carry out a development project must obtain planning permission from the local authority in the area. To accommodate concern about the environment, an important new step has been introduced into the planning process. In February 1990, the EC Directive on Environmental Impact Assessments (EIA) finally became law in the Republic. A similar law was introduced in 1989 in Northern Ireland. The Directive states that major development proposals, including mining, need to be accompanied by an Environmental Impact Statement (EIS) when planning and permission is being sought. The EIS has to examine the environmental impact of the proposed development as well as the plans for dealing with any negative consequences. A planning decision made by the local authority can be submitted to the Planning Appeals Board, which was established in 1977.

Sanitary authorities, usually the county or city councils, have a wide range of functions relating to air, water, pollution, sewage, water supply, waste disposal and suppression of nuisance. Most of these are key areas of environmental stress in Ireland and, as such, the local authorities' role in protecting the environment has been closely examined by environmental groups. The larger local authorities also have responsibility for the protection of the quality of water under the Local Government (Water Pollution) Act 1977 and the Local Government (Water Pollution) (Amendment) Act 1990.

Despite the responsibilities of the local authorities, however, the Minister of the Environment monitors the actions of local authorities and can exercise a good deal of power in relation to their activities. Furthermore, because of their dependence on central government finance, local authorities are very dependent on the Department of the Environment. Thus the implementation – as well as the formulation – of policy with respect to the environment is highly centralised, a state of affairs that may be consolidated when the Environmental Protection Agency (EPA) comes into operation.

As part of an attempt to address the *ad hoc* nature of Irish environmental policy, as well as handle the volume and complexity of EC environmental legislation, the government has recently established a new body, the Environmental Protection Agency. According to the Department of the Environment, a number of factors have contributed to the establishment of the EPA, including:

- the need to reform the administrative structures responsible for pollution control to take account of new responsibilities and priorities;
- the depth and breadth of new environmental legislation, especially that originating from the EC;
- the increased inability of local authorities to implement these new regulations, especially in relation to the increasingly sophisticated nature of industrial and commercial activity;
- the lack of environmental and specific expertise by local authorities; the loss of public confidence in the ability of the administration to ensure effective pollution control; and the slow down in industrial development as a consequence of campaigns by environmental groups.

The Department hopes that the establishment of the EPA will restore public confidence in the ability of the state to protect the environment in the face of commercial and industrial activity. They believe the EPA can achieve this by:

- establishing a body of expertise in the areas of environmental management, especially pollution control;
- aiding the local authorities in their tasks of pollution control;
- centralising specific functions, especially those of a more complex or technical nature; and
- developing an integrated approach towards pollution control.

The EPA will act as a kind of 'controlling agent' overseeing the work of local authorities. It is also envisaged that it will take on some direct pollution control tasks, as well as take over some of the duties that the local authorities currently hold. It will have powers to monitor the state of the environment and oversee the implementation of environmental legislation. The EPA will also issue licences, under a system called 'Integrated Pollution Control Licensing', to industry in respect of waste disposal, pollution of the air and water, and noise pollution.

For years environmental groups, especially Earthwatch, have been calling for the establishment of a national agency to take charge of environmental protection. However, environmentalists have expressed their concern about the level of independence that the new agency will be allowed to have, how adequate its funding will be, and whether it will be allowed to examine all aspects of economic activity, rather than being narrowly focused upon the environmental consequences of industrial activity.

As well as central, regional and local governmental involve-ment in environmental matters, state-sponsored bodies also exist. Many of these act as monitoring and advisory agencies. Included among these state-sponsored bodies is the Wildlife Service, a branch of the Office of Public Works. This is involved in the conservation of wild flora and fauna and their habitats. Teagasc, the Agricultural and Food Development Authority, is another such body and it undertakes research relating to agriculture and the food industry.

One of the main agencies charged with monitoring the state of the Irish environment is Eolas. Eolas, the Irish Science and Technology Agency, is an organisation that was formed in 1987 from the Institute for Industrial Research and Standards as well as the National Board for Science and Technology. Eolas provides services to industry in such areas as information technology, construction technology, energy and the environment. One of Eolas' chief tasks is to certify that products and services meet national and international standards, for example, for safety.

In 1987, An Foras Forbartha was abolished by the govern-ment. This body had been responsible for providing advice and research on physical planning and development as well as water resources. However, in 1988, the government established the

Environmental Research Unit (EUR), under the Department of the Environment. As a consequence of its location within the Department, the EUR lacks autonomy and thus differs in a major respect from its predecessor, An Foras Forbartha. It is responsible for the provision of environmental research and advice with regard to infrastructural developments and the environment. Its main activities fall within seven areas of work: road traffic, safety and transport; road construction and transport; water resources; environmental services; construction; planning; environmental awareness and the provision of a library service. As part of its work, for example, the EUR published a handbook for sanitary authorities to help them implement EC directives regarding drinking water quality.

Another important new step has been the establishment of ENFO: Environmental Information Services, an information centre designed to provide up-to-date information on all aspects of Irish environmental law and practices. Strictly speaking, ENFO is part of the Department of the Environment, reporting directly to its Environment Division. Furthermore, most of the staff are employed directly by the Department. However, the government has been concerned to ensure that ENFO portrays an image of autonomy. Thus its offices are located in a separate building, it has its own budget and it exercises autonomy on day-to-day decision-making.

An Taisce is a unique environmental group in Ireland. Although not a governmental organisation, it is what is known as a 'prescribed' organisation. As a prescribed organisation, planning authorities are obliged by law to send An Taisce copies of their development plans, as well as planning applications in areas of special amenities. It can be regarded as the watch-dog of the Irish planning process and as the protector of the national heritage.

Northern Ireland Partly as a consequence of the increased involvement of the EC in the area of environmental issues, a number of important new laws have also come into force in Northern Ireland. The main pieces of legislation, known as 'orders in Council', dealing with the countryside and wildlife in Northern Ireland were all introduced in the mid-1980s. These include the Access to the Countryside (Northern Ireland) Order 1983, the Wildlife (Northern Ireland) Order 1985 and the Nature Conservation and Amenity Lands (Northern Ireland) Order 1985. The first of these concerns access to the countryside by, for example, hikers and ramblers. The second is concerned with the provision of species protection and the third with the provision of habitat protection and conservation of scenic areas.

The Department of the Environment in Northern Ireland has the main responsibility for both conservation and environmental protection:

- Town and Country Planning Service
- the Countryside and Wildlife Branch
- Environmental Protection Division
- Landscape Division and
- Water Service.

Since Direct Rule was introduced in 1972, however, there has been a tendency for a single Minister to hold responsibility for more than one department and it is rare for a Minister to have sole responsibility for the Department of the Environment. Furthermore, the Minister's Under-Secretary can hold many responsibilities, and the present Under-Secretary in the Department of the Environment represents the Conservation Service, the Environmental Protection Division, the Housing Division and the section dealing with local government. This burden of responsibility can only serve to diminish the importance given to environmental conservation and protection in Northern Ireland.

Planning, a chief responsibility of the Republic's local authorities, is carried out in Northern Ireland by the Department of the Environment's Town and Country Planning Service, which is split into six divisions and has Divisional Planning Offices in the main towns. A major part of the Town and

Country Planning Service's work is the preparation of 'Development Plans', which establish guidelines for future planning. Once a development plan is prepared it is made available for public scrutiny and, if there are a number of objections to the plan, a public inquiry can be held. Recently, a public inquiry into the Omagh Area Development Plan was held, where local, national and international environmental groups voiced their objections to the development of gold mining in the region.

The Town and Country Planning Service is responsible for granting planning permission. Any person proposing to carry out a development project must, as in the Republic, apply for planning permission at the nearest Divisional Planning Office. Sometimes if the proposed project is of a controversial nature or is likely to have major environmental or conservation implications the Planning Office can refer the application to headquarters in Belfast. If planning permission is rejected then an appeal can be made to the Planning Appeals Commission.

The Department of the Environment in Northern Ireland has a Conservation Service and this has two main branches: the Countryside and Wildlife Branch and the Historic Monuments and Buildings Branch. The function of the Countryside and Wildlife Branch is to protect the best natural and unspoiled areas of Northern Ireland. This is done by establishing:

1 Areas of Special Scientific Interest (ASSIs). An ASSI is an area that is recognised as an internationally, nationally or regionally important site for nature conservation and is, therefore, protected against damaging land use. The Nature Conservation and Amenity Lands (Northern Ireland) Order 1985 governs the establishment of ASSIs. ASSIs include bogs, woodlands and meadows and since 1986 twenty-three ASSIs have been declared by the Department.

2 National Nature Reserve (NNR). NNRs are sites that represent the best examples of habitat existing in Northern Ireland. They are managed either to conserve nature or for education and research purposes. Many are open to the public and a total of forty-five now exist. No marine

nature reserves have been established, but negotiations are in progress for the establishment of one in Strangford Lough, as it is considered to be of exceptional scientific and wildlife interest.

3   Areas of Outstanding Natural Beauty (AONBs). AONBs are larger than either ASSIs or NNRs and they have broader objectives. An area is declared an AONB to either conserve or enhance the natural beauty or amenity of an area, to conserve wildlife and historic objects, or to promote its enjoyment by the public. The Mourne Mountains, the Glens of Antrim and the Antrim Coast, as well as the Giant's Causeway coast, are AONBs. The Giant's Causeway is also a World Heritage Site.

4   Country parks and countryside centres. Country parks are designed to promote enjoyment of the countryside and provide facilities such as camp sites and nature trails. Seven such parks exist in Northern Ireland, as well as three countryside centres that provide visitors with information, exhibitions and displays on aspects of the local countryside. The parks and centres are staffed by nature wardens and rangers.

In undertaking its work the Department of the Environment consults with the Council for Nature Conservation and the Countryside, a body that helps it to formulate policy on nature conservation. However, as this body only had its first meeting in June 1989 it is too early to assess its impact on environmental policy in Northern Ireland. Despite its seemingly impressive list of activities, environmental groups have been critical of the Department's conservation record, for example, for failing to establish wildlife refuges, for designating far too few sites for special protection, especially the designation of ASSIs. Environmentalists have also been very critical of the administration of conservation policy in Northern Ireland. In particular, they accuse the government of failing to provide an adequate structure, funding and staff to administer conservation and have repeatedly called for the establishment of a statutory conservation agency that would be independent of the Department of the Environment.

The Environmental Protection Division of the Department is responsible for a wide range of functions relating to environmental protection, including waste management, noise control, clean air systems, food inspection and consumer protection. The Division also provides advice on disposal methods for hazardous and toxic waste. These activities are covered by laws and the Division is responsible for ensuring the implementation of a number of laws concerned with public health and pollution control, including the Pollution Control and the Local Government (Northern Ireland) Order 1987, Food and Environment Protection Act 1985, Control of Pollution Act 1974, Water Act 1972 and the Clean Air (Northern Ireland) Order 1981. In order to help it in these tasks the Division works closely with local public health officers and rivers inspectors.

A major tasks of the Division is the control of discharges to inland and coastal waterways. As part of this, the Division monitors water quality in rivers, and currently has 138 monitoring stations throughout Northern Ireland. It also initiates prosecutions of those suspected of waterway pollution and organises preventive action and cleaning up in pollution emergencies. The Division is also responsible for developing general policy on waste disposal, as well as implementing EC waste disposal legislation.

Other Departments are also involved in environmental protection. The Department of Agriculture's Water Drainage and Conservation Division has responsibility for all environmental matters relating to farmland. The Department is also involved in the designation of Environmentally Sensitive Areas, where farmers in areas of particular conservation importance have agreed to a five-year conservation plan in exchange for financial payments. The Department's Forest Service is responsible for most land under forest in Northern Ireland. The Department of Economic Development also has environmental responsibilities; for example, the Minerals and Petroleum Branch issues prospecting and mining licences.

Unlike the Republic, local authorities in Northern Ireland do not have a major role to play in environmental protection or nature conservation. When Direct Rule was introduced, authorities lost powers over such areas as planning, water supply and roads. These are now handled by central government. One function that local authorities do have is responsibility for the implementation of the Access to the Countryside Order. District councils also have power under the Nature Conservation and Amenity Land Order to establish and manage local nature reserves, and while the record of some councils has been excellent, most have done very little by way of nature conservation work.

District councils have responsibility for actual waste management and they therefore collect and dispose of domestic and commercial waste. Recycling facilities are also provided by district councils, including the provision of can and bottle banks. The councils also run schemes for the removal of CFCs from old refrigerators. Under the Pollution Control and Local Government (Northern Ireland) Order 1978 councils can initiate prosecutions for littering and illegal dumping. However, while the district councils have the responsibility for the disposal of waste, it is the Environmental Protection Division of the Department of the Environment that takes charge of developing waste disposal policies and that is responsible for implementing EC legislation on waste disposal.

As in the Republic, most refuse is disposed of in landfills. Belfast Lough and Lough Foyle have been used extensively for this purpose. However, there is a considerable amount of illegal dumping, especially on the side of the road and in marshy land.

Conclusion

It is clear that economic development, modernisation and urbanisation continue to bring new pressures to bear upon the natural environment. In response to the increased public concern about these environmental pressures many new developments have occurred within the whole area of environmental policy in Ireland. Chief among these has been the introduction of new laws that not only tighten legislation but also widen the scope of environmental protection. New environmental protection bodies have been established and new planning procedures introduced, including the introduction of EIAs into the planning process. Future changes are also expected, especially as the EC widens and deepens its involvement in environmental protection.

Environmental protection is a complex issue and it does not just involve the provision of adequate laws and regulatory agencies. Consideration of deeper issues of a social as well as economic nature is also required. Those concerned with finding a deep and lasting solution to the environmental crisis will have to move beyond 'quick fix' technological solutions to a more fundamental appraisal of the way in which we interact with the natural world, and ultimately, with each other.

References

Gormley, J. (1990), *The Green Guide for Ireland*, Wolfhound Press, Dublin.

Earthwatch (1989), *Salmon Farming in Ireland: Environmental and Legislative Problems Assessed*, Special Report no. 4, Bantry.

An Foras Forbartha (1985), *The State of the Environment*, An Foras Forbartha, Dublin.

Index